MARITIME STRATEGY, GEOPOLITICS, AND THE DEFENSE OF THE WEST

MARITIME STRATEGY, GEOPOLITICS, AND THE DEFENSE OF THE WEST

COLIN S. GRAY

NATIONAL STRATEGY INFORMATION CENTER, INC.

Maritime Strategy, Geopolitics, and the Defense of the West

Published in the United States by

Ramapo Press
363 Seventh Ave.
New York, NY 10001

Copyright © 1986 National Strategy Information Center, Inc.
150 East 58th Street
New York, NY 10155

Library of Congress Catalog Card Number 86-62424

Library of Congress Cataloging-in-Publication Data

Gray, Colin S.
    Maritime strategy, geopolitics, and the defense of the West.

    Bibliography: p.
    1. Sea-power—United States   2. United States—
National security.   I. Title.
VA50.G73 1986   359'.03'0973   86-62424
ISBN 0-915071-02-9

Printed in the United States of America

TABLE OF CONTENTS

PREFACE

In 1977, NSIC published its all-time best selling monograph by a young British-born defense analyst and scholar on the then-forbidding topic of "geopolitics," the unalterable relation between geography and strategic power. Colin Gray's *The Geopolitics of the Nuclear Era* was not only a masterful review of the great theorists of the pre-atomic age such as Mahan and Mackinder. The author also manifestly succeeded in his wish that contemporary political scientists would be encouraged "by this study . . . to examine their culturally-bequeathed mental world maps, and consider the global policy implications . . . of the Soviet military buildup of the 1970s."

Nine years later, due in no small part to Dr. Gray's efforts, geopolitics is no longer an obscure "buzzword" in the lexicon of professional defense mavens; but the author has rendered another unique service by updating our strategic maps with refined coordinates and new dimensions. Persons well versed in security matters can talk easily about MX missiles, laser research, or the probable effect of a "no first use" policy on the morale of the NATO allies. They are much less likely to discuss the importance to Western defense of the Strait of Hormuz or the Yucatan Channel. Glamorous weapons are more publicized than obscure choke points, although the latter may have more bearing on ultimate victory in global war. The size and quality of armies are more "interesting" than the means and routes by which they must be supplied or reinforced.

History celebrates the dashing combat commander, not the naval architect or the construction engineer. Who would not prefer to be a hero of "maneuver" stratagems than the drudge obliged to help an army move on its stomach? There is little romance in logistics, and no Victoria Cross for genius in the transportation corps. Yet, whatever the skill and valor of a general, military power must perforce be projected through, across, or around intractable geography. That this central discipline is still slighted in civilian universities and even war colleges is ample reason to rejoice in Colin Gray's new treatise.

This gifted scholar has the singular ability to master and explicate a wealth of technical data while, at the same time, keeping the reader grounded in the principles of a unifying grand strategy, of which the "maritime" and the "continental" comprise complementary parts. He rightly perforates the false dichotomy of "seapower versus landpower." Indeed, he is one of the few defense experts to perceive that a workable SDI, superior fleets in being, sterling ground forces, and diplomatic finesse are synergistic imperatives, not competitive options.

His roadmap of modern geopolitics not only details the ocean thruways to critical raw materials and forward bases, but illuminates the less visible psychopolitical networks that sustain Alliance esprit. Perhaps we can never be reminded often enough that, while Mother Russia is contiguous to its Eastern European satellites, great oceans separate the United States from its allies in Europe, Japan, Israel, and Australia. The disparate "islands" of the free world have, collectively, a decisive edge in manpower and GNP over the Warsaw Pact; but those fragmented assets can only be connected by unsubduable maritime strength.

Dr. Gray brings the same analytical acuity to the study of naval strategy and landpower that he did to nuclear forces in the earlier work. His historically-based and policy oriented observations clearly demonstrate the true synergy of land, sea, and aerospace capabilities in a multilateral, defensive coalition that only the United States can lead in this high-tech era.

Colin S. Gray was educated at the universities of Manchester and Oxford, and has taught at various universities in the United Kingdom and Canada. He was Assistant Director of the International Institute for Strategic Studies, and was Director of National Security Studies at the Hudson Institute. Since 1981 Dr. Gray has been President of the National Institute for Public Policy in Fairfax, Virginia. His recent publications include *Strategic Studies and Public Policy: The American Experience* (1982); *American Military Space Policy* (1983); and *Nuclear Strategy and National Style* (1986). Dr. Gray recently concluded a major study of *Geopolitics, Strategic Culture, and National Security,* and is currently working on studies of strategy and the relationship between seapower and landpower.

Frank R. Barnett, President
National Strategy Information Center, Inc.
August 1986

I do not say the Frenchman will not come;
I only say he will not come by sea.

Lord St. Vincent, in 1803,
on the prospects for a French
invasion of Great Britain

From the days when humans first began to use the seas, the
great lesson of history is that the enemy who is confined to a
land strategy is in the end defeated.

Field Marshal Viscount Montgomery
of Alamein

INTRODUCTION:
THE RENAISSANCE
IN US MARITIME
STRATEGY

The most frequent and damaging of charges leveled at the US military establishment is that it has no strategy. Indeed, a very important stimulus to the contemporary flurry of "military reform" activities is precisely the concern that the Reagan Administration has been throwing money at ill-analyzed defense problems, with no "strategy police" determining and effecting priorities.[1] The charge is demonstrably wide of the mark with reference to the US Navy. As Norman Friedman reminds us,[2] for the first time since 1945 the Navy has an explicit maritime strategy that specifies goals, guides procurement decisions, and, in the Navy's words, makes a strategic difference.[3]

---

[1] For example, see US Congress, Senate Committee on Armed Services, *Defense Organization: The Need for Change,* Staff Report, 99th Cong., 1st sess. (Washington, DC: US Government Printing Office, October 16, 1985), pp. 15, 81–82, 622–24, 637.

[2] Norman Friedman, "US Maritime Strategy," *International Defense Review,* vol. 18, no. 7 (1985), pp. 1071–75; and "Comment and Discussion: 'Northern Flank Maritime Offensive'," US Naval Institute *Proceedings,* vol. 112/2/996 (February 1986), particularly p. 25.

[3] The Maritime Strategy is described in considerable detail in the US Navy briefing presented in US Congress, House Committee on Armed Services, Subcommittee on Seapower, *The 600 Ship Navy, Hearings,* 99th Cong., 1st sess. (Washington, DC: US Government Printing Office, forthcoming). (Hereafter referred to as "600 Ship Navy Briefing"); and Admiral James D. Watkins et al., *The Maritime Strategy,* Supplement to *Proceedings,* vol. 112/1/996 (January 1986).

One of the benefits of an indeterminacy in strategy is that potential critics are deprived of specific targets to assault. With its explicit Maritime Strategy, the US Navy inevitably has provided targets for a wide range of critics.[4] Behind the charges and responses lurks the potential for a "great debate" over the character of US, and US-allied, global strategy. Quite properly, and in contradiction of some of the critics, the Maritime Strategy is a coalition-supportive design that fits well within a fairly optimistic view of the likely course of an East-West military conflict. Should deterrence fail, the Navy would have a three-fold mission: to protect the sea lines of communication; to take pressure off the Central Front in Europe; and to press the Soviet Union, world-wide, on the maritime flanks of its continental imperium.[5]

Central to this monograph is the view that the United States is a continental-size insular power, which is able to secure a working command of the most strategically relevant sea lines of communication. Moreover, the United States can knit together a maritime alliance that includes the lion's share of the gross world product. Most of the world, even around peripheral Eurasia, is not easily accessible to Soviet tank armies.[6] Depending on how one performs the accounting, the maritime alliance led by the United States has an economic advantage over the Warsaw Pact on the order of three- or four-to-one.

Notwithstanding its economic potential for defense mobilization, the West continues to permit itself the luxury of a defense posture and strategy in Europe that is relatively cheap in peacetime, but whose scale of nuclear dependency most likely would confront NATO governments with intolerable choices shortly after the onset of hostilities.[7] The Maritime Strategy, as typically portrayed, is both

---

[4] Among the more thoughtful is John M. Collins. See his list of questions in "Comment and Discussion: The Maritime Strategy," US Naval Institute *Proceedings*, vol. 112/3/997 (March 1986), pp. 18, 20, 22. The Navy's answers to Collins are provided by Rear Admiral William Pendley in "Comment and Discussion: 'The Maritime Strategy'," US Naval Institute Proceedings, vol. 112/6/1000 (June 1986), pp. 84, 86, 88–89.

[5] "600 Ship Navy Briefing."

[6] Even in Western Europe, with its dense road network, a Soviet invasion would be canalized by urban areas and by forested and hilly terrain. See John J. Mearsheimer, *Conventional Deterrence* (Ithaca, NY: Cornell University Press, 1983), Chapter 6.

[7] This prospect has been stated and restated very plainly by NATO's Supreme Allied Commander, Europe (SACEUR), General Bernard Rogers. See Rogers, "Greater Flexibility for

defended and assailed in terms of a NATO strategy of flexible response that envisages only a relatively brief conflict. The US Navy is constrained to argue both that it could make an important strategic difference to the outcome of a short war, and that it would most certainly have a prospectively decisive impact upon the course and outcome of a long war. At the present time, however, it is difficult to argue plausibly that NATO would be able to hold long enough for maritime pressure to have an important effect upon the contest.

What would happen were NATO to lose a ground war in Europe in a matter of days, weeks, or perhaps even months as ammunition, equipment, and reasonably ready reservists were expended? Current NATO strategy identifies the US strategic nuclear forces as the "extended deterrent" of the alliance.[8] Should the ground war in Europe proceed badly, the alliance would expect the United States —with its enormous political, military, economic, and human, investment in Europe—to engage in controlled vertical (nuclear) escalation in pursuit of a satisfactory, early termination of the war. For obvious reasons, the allies in Europe may well prove to be as reluctant to sanction nuclear use in their defense as would a US President to initiate a central war in the hope of persuading a victory-flushed Soviet leadership to return to the territorial *status quo ante.*

What has happened is that NATO has elected to gamble on the continuing deterrent efficacy of awesome nuclear threats, in the belief that the Soviet Union does not need very much deterring in the 1980s and beyond. The nuclear escalation threat that is critical to the alliance's authoritative strategic concept of flexible and controlled response is applicable only by the side that has, in the words of the late Herman Kahn, "escalation dominance."[9] In short, it is a concept appropriate only for the strategically superior (or the very reckless).[10]

NATO's Flexible Response," *Strategic Review,* vol. XI, no. 2 (Spring 1983), pp. 11–19; and "Keep that gap from getting any bigger," *US News and World Report,* January 20, 1986, p. 26. For a sensibly equivocal judgment, see *The Military Balance, 1985–1986* (London: International Institute for Strategic Studies, 1985), p. 185.

[8] See Walter Slocombe, "Extended Deterrence," *The Washington Quarterly,* vol. 7, no. 4 (Fall 1984), pp. 93–103.

[9] Herman Kahn, *On Escalation: Metaphors and Scenarios* (New York: Praeger, 1965), p. 290.

[10] This is not to deny that NATO would have the "defender's advantage" and should be presumed to be willing to take higher risks to preserve its territorial (and hence political) integrity than would the Soviet Union to secure gain. Nonetheless, too much comfort should

There is a slow drift towards a substantially, if not wholly, alternative strategic policy design for the United States and the Eurasian rimland coalition that it leads. Specifically, the "extended deterrent" of the West, instead of comprising the nuclear sword, rather should be the defense mobilization potential of an alliance that commands the world's oceans and hence can maneuver on a global scale to achieve superiority in places and at times of its choosing. Needless to say, the defense mobilization potential of the Western (and some Asian) economies requires protection against both short-war defeat on the ground in a critical theater — preeminently Central-Western Europe — and short-war defeat via Soviet nuclear escalation.

This is not to suggest that extant US policy for its strategic forces is unsound. On the contrary, given the possible strength of the Soviet incentive to escalate out of an impending global protracted war, the United States and its allies will need every ounce of dissuasive effect that can be gleaned from strategic offensive and defensive forces capable of denying the Soviet Union, on its own terms of strategic-cultural reference, some facsimile of victory.[11] Furthermore, the belated US endorsement of strategic defense could assist greatly in "fencing off" the US homeland and its military mobilization potential from violent assault by a Soviet Union frustrated elsewhere.[12] In addition, and quite contrary to the allegations of many critics, a maritime emphasis in US global strategy would not detract from the strategic importance and local military needs of NATO. One should not need to enlist the services of a latter-day Carl von Clausewitz or Julian Corbett in order to recognize that it would be vitally important for Soviet military power to be massively "distracted," and ground down, by active continental campaigning —thereby reducing critically the Soviet ability to garrison and reinforce its distant flanks.

This monograph argues that the United States is, first and

---

not be drawn from the nominal "defender's advantage," both because at issue is the credibility of US strategic nuclear action on behalf of distant allies, and because a Soviet Union sufficiently motivated as to invade NATO-Europe should be presumed to be sufficiently motivated as not to be readily discouraged in pursuit of its goals.

[11] Issues of nuclear strategy, in cultural perspective, are treated at length in Colin S. Gray, *Nuclear Strategy and National Style* (Lanham, MD: Hamilton Press, 1986).

[12] See Keith B. Payne, "The Deterrence Requirement for Defense," *The Washington Quarterly*, vol. 9, no. 1 (Winter 1986), pp. 139–54.

foremost, a sea power. Strategic air and missile power, in the absence of a very convincing capability to limit damage through offensive and defensive counterforce, must responsibly be regarded as a counterdeterrent, not as a reliable equalizer for theater defense deficiencies. It is argued in these pages that a maritime emphasis in overall US national military strategy makes sense, whether or not one believes that NATO can hold, somewhere, on the ground in Central-Western Europe.

A great American strategic theorist, J.C. Wylie, has written that "planning for certitude is the greatest of all military mistakes, as military history demonstrates all too vividly."[13] In keeping with Wylie's advice, the author recognizes that there is, and can be, no certitude over NATO's continental defense prospects or over the likelihood of nuclear escalation. On occasion, as can happen in the heat of debate, spokesmen for the US Navy have described a strategic context replete with self-serving assumptions (e.g., no nuclear use, a long war) regarding the effectiveness of maritime activity. It is suggested here that, properly conceived and related to strategic-nuclear forces and to landpower, the Navy's Maritime Strategy speaks to Western strengths rather than to Western weaknesses, can provide for continental failure or success, and should be the offensive centerpiece of US national security policy in an environment of strategic-nuclear parity and theater-nuclear inferiority.

In important respects this monograph should be viewed as an extension of *The Geopolitics of the Nuclear Era,* published in 1977.[14] That study emphasized the ideas of the great geopolitical theorists and stressed the character and weight of the Soviet-Heartland challenged to the Rimlands of Eurasia and the maritime alliance led by the United States. This monograph does not seek, generally, to repeat very much of the theoretical exposition of the earlier work. Instead it provides extensive discussion of the landpower-seapower opposition and, in particular, focuses upon the implications of East-West geopolitical relationships for the design of US national military strategy (a subject treated very lightly in the 1977 work).

---

[13] J.C. Wylie, *Military Strategy: A General Theory of Power Control* (Westport, CT: Greenwood Press, 1980; first pub. 1967), p. 85.

[14] Colin S. Gray, *The Geopolitics of the Nuclear Era: Heartland, Rimlands, and the Technological Revolution.* (New York: Crane Russak, on behalf of the National Strategy Information Center, 1977).

1

GEOPOLITICS
AND SEAPOWER

Geopolitics is a much abused term, often employed simply to add portentousness to a text — as they say in the movie industry, it sounds like "high concept." What is geopolitics? A truly authoritative definition is lacking, but two offerings, written twenty-two years apart, provide insights useful for the purposes of this discussion. Writing in 1942, Robert Strausz-Hupé advised that:

> This global scheme of political strategy [elaborated by German theorists in the 1920s] is geopolitics . . . . geopolitics is the master plan that tells what and why to conquer, guiding the military strategist along the easiest path to conquest.[1]

Not only did Adolf Hitler lack a scheme of conquest worthy of description as a "master plan," but his objectives and his methods after 1938 were very far short of masterly. In 1967, Saul B. Cohen provided a vastly more neutral definition when he said that geopolitics refers to "the relation of international political power to the geographical setting."[2]

German *Geopolitik* was viewed in the United States in the early 1940s as having provided detailed guidance for Hitler's statecraft.

---

[1] Robert Strausz-Hupé, *Geopolitics: The Struggle for Space and Power* (New York: Arno, 1972; first pub. 1942), p. vii.
[2] Saul B. Cohen, *Geography and Politics in a Divided World* (London: Methuen, 1964), p. 24.

This was a somewhat fanciful proposition on the part of American theorists of international relations, and it did not long survive the demise of the Third Reich (though the leading German geopolitical theorist, Karl Haushofer, was considered for arraignment as a war criminal at Nuremberg.)[3] Geopolitics went out of fashion in the United States for nearly forty years, for three reasons: it was as- sociated with German *Geopolitik,* American politicans were not comfortable with grand theory, and it transcended treatment by the evolving methodologies of the American ''scientific'' study of in- ternational relations.[4]

It is a premise of this monograph that an understanding of the geographical setting of Soviet-American security relations — the problems and opportunities provided by geography—should com- prise a critically important input for the making of US national security policy and its derivative national military strategy. Most of the more insightful writings on the shelves of twentieth century geopolitical theory have focused on the theme of ''landpower versus seapower.''[5] The landpower-seapower opposition remains relevant in the latter years of this century, notwithstanding the invention and evolution of the airplane, nuclear weapons, ballistic missiles, orbital spacecraft, and near-instantaneous global communications.[6] The strategic danger to insular maritime Britain, from the birth of the modern state system in the sixteenth century to the present day, has always been the prospect of a country or coalition of countries on

---

[3] See Edmund A. Walsh, S.J., *Total Power: A Footnote to History* (Garden City, NY: Doubleday, 1949), Chapters 1–6. Father Walsh interrogated Dr. Karl Haushofer extensively in October-November 1945. Also valuable are Strausz-Hupé, *Geopolitics;* Andreas Dorpalen, *The World of General Haushofer: Geopolitics in Action* (Port Washington, NY: Kenikat, 1966; first pub. 1942); and Derwent Whittlesey, ''Haushofer: The Geopoliticians,'' in Edward Mead Earle, ed., *Makers of Modern Strategy: Military Thought from Machiavelli to Hitler* (Princeton, NJ: Princeton University Press, 1941), Chapter 16; and Jean Klein, ''Reflections on Geopolitics: From Pangermanism to the Doctrines of Living Space and Moving Frontiers,'' in Ciro Zoppo and Charles Zorgbibe, eds., *On Geopolitics: Classical and Nuclear* (Dordrecht: Martinus Nijhoff, 1985), pp. 45–75.

[4] A collection of first-rate essays, commissioned by NATO's Scientific Affairs Division, is evidence of some revival of interest: Zoppo and Zorgbibe, eds., *On Geopolitics.*

[5] Effectively beginning with Halford J. Mackinder, *Democratic Ideals and Reality* (New York: Norton, 1962). This volume contains entries that span more than forty years in dates of authorship. See also James Trapier Lowe, *Geopolitics and War: Mackinder's Philosophy of Power* (Washington, DC: University Press of America, 1981), Chapter 2.

[6] A view endorsed in George Liska, ''From Containment To Concert,'' *Foreign Policy,* no. 62 (Spring 1986), pp. 3–23.

the continent achieving so unchallenged a position of relative strength in landpower, that it or they would be at liberty to organize the great resources of the continent for the purpose of gaining a preponderant position at sea. *Ab extensio* to a far wider geographical canvas, this same logic mandated American intervention in World Wars I and II, and is the rationale for the Eurasian on-shore global containment policy pursued with variable vigor since the late 1940s.

The US alliance systems with NATO-Europe and with Japan (and the functional equivalent of alliance with the Chinese People's Republic), all serve to keep the Soviet Union essentially in a land-locked condition. Soviet power projection beyond Eurasia could be effected only on Western sufferance, given that the maritime alliance led by the United States controls the chokepoints that Soviet sea-power must transit if it is to be loose on the high seas.[7] Western sufferance may be secured by virtue of the hostage status of Western assets contiguous to Soviet landpower, and may in minor key be evaded by overflight. Still, the ability of the Soviet Union to conduct armed adventure in pursuit of *Weltpolitik* is effectively checkable today by the United States' and allied control of the "Rimland" geography of Eurasia, just as Germany's ability to act as a world power was controllable by the British Royal Navy.[8]

A key to the development of potentially preponderant seapower is a hinterland for naval bases either inaccessible to hostile land-power, or which is unchallenged due to a successful hegemonic policy. The continental-landpower traditions of Germany and Rus-sia/the Soviet Union were, and remain, the products of necessity.

---

[7] For a sense of déjà vu, see Alfred T. Mahan, *Retrospect and Prospect: Studies in International Relations, Naval and Political* (London: Sampson Low, Marston, 1902; first pub. 1901), pp. 139–205.

[8] "The Continent of Europe can engage in distant naval operations only with the consent of Britain, not against her." Nicholas John Spykman, *America's Strategy in World Politics: The United States and the Balance of Power* (Hamden, CT: Archon Books, 1970; first pub. 1942), p. 98. Spykman developed the "Rimland" concept in his book (published posthumously), *The Geography of the Peace* (New York: Harcourt, Brace, 1944). For an interesting critique of Spykman's theories and policy advice (US intervention to deny Germany control of a "United Eurasia"), see Michael Vlahos, *America: Images of Empire*, Occasional Papers in International Affairs (Washington, DC: School of Advanced International Studies, Johns Hopkins Foreign Policy Institute, August 1982), pp. 51–58. A detailed recent appraisal of Spykman is David Wilkinson, "Spykman and Geopolitics," in Zoppo and Zorgbibe, eds., *On Geopolitics,* pp. 77–129. *Weltpolitik* refers to the assertion of the role of world power. See Woodruff D. Smith, *The Ideological Origins of Nazi Imperialism* (New York: Oxford University Press, 1986), Chapter 4.

Neither Germany nor Russia has secured, or even come close to securing, the major continental landpower preeminence sufficient for a wholehearted bid for achievement of superior maritime power. However, any Americans in the 1980s who are attracted to the idea of cutting and running from the nuclear dangers inherent in the Eurasian containment perimeter should be given pause by a little historical reflection. Imperial Germany, facing the admitted certainty of a land war on two fronts, still found the resources to build a "luxury fleet" that was within qualitative and quantitative reach of the Royal Navy by 1914.[9] More to the point perhaps, a Soviet Union that suffers from virtually every possible disadvantage with respect to the development and prospective employment of maritime power has constructed a very formidable Navy.

Had there been no "miracle of the Marne" in the second week of September 1914, it is entirely possible that the Kaiser's High Seas Fleet would have been augmented to the point where Great Britain would have been obliged to acquiesce in a German hegemony. Looking to the next century, if the Soviet Union no longer has to prepare for major land war in Europe and Asia, even the monumental thirty-year achievement of Admiral Gorshkov[10] would pale by comparison with what an expanded Soviet imperium could assemble by way of a maritime challenge to the United States. This is the strategic logic of geopolitics most relevant to this discussion. However, it has to be a matter for speculation the extent to which the junior standing of the Navy among the Soviet armed services, and the continentalist strategic culture of the most influential members of those services, might serve as a persisting brake upon Soviet naval policy—almost regardless of the context of geopolitical opportunity. This author is very respectful of the argument that the Russian/Soviet strategic world view is fundamentally that of the landsman, but is no less respectful of Soviet ability to shift priorities according to geostrategic circumstances.[11]

---

[9] Among a truly vast literature see: Holger H. Herwig, *"Luxury Fleet": The Imperial German Navy, 1888–1918* (London: Allen and Unwin, 1980); Ivo N. Lambi, *The Navy and German Power Politics, 1862–1914* (London: Allen and Unwin, 1984); and Paul M. Kennedy, "Strategic Aspects of the Anglo-German Naval Race," in Kennedy, *Strategy and Diplomacy, 1870–1945: Eight Studies* (London: Allen and Unwin, 1983), pp. 127–60.

[10] See Harlan K. Ullman, "Dosvidonya Sergei," *Sea Power,* vol. 29, no. 2 (February 1986), pp. 13–15.

[11] For some necessary historical perspective, see Donald W. Mitchell, *A History of Russian and Soviet Sea Power* (London: Andre Deutsch, 1974).

2

STRATEGIC GEOGRAPHY
AND THE STRUCTURE
OF US SECURITY

AMERICAN INSULARITY AND THE MARITIME ALLIANCE

To understand the security problems and opportunities of the United States, one has to begin with geography—political, physical, economic, cultural. In the most direct terms, the United States is an effectively insular super-state and the principal organizer and only possible leader of a truly global maritime alliance. With custom-designed and suitably eccentric cartography—"magic maps"—one can demonstrate the plausibility of virtually any geopolitical theory. However, it is no exaggeration to claim that the United States occupies essentially a central geographical position *vis à vis* regions of great security interest, and that the oceanic trade (and power projection) routes of the world are the lines of internal communication of the US-led maritime alliance.

Although the United States occupies a central position with respect to lines of communication to Eurasia, it is no less true that the Soviet Union—occupying the Eurasian Heartland—holds a central position and has advantageous interior lines of communication *vis à vis* much, though far from all, of Eurasia. The concepts of interior lines of communication and depth of territory or sea for defense do not lend themselves mechanistically to easy and automatic translation to military advantage. Japan discovered that distance, or depth, can mean weakness, if reliance is placed upon far-flung and static garrisons insufficiently supported by powerful mobile strike forces. In the absence of fleet superiority, the Japanese concept of a far distant defensive barrier was a prescription for disaster.[1]

The Heartland position of the Soviet state looks very menacing indeed regarding the Eurasian Rimland arc of US security clients ranging from Norway around to South Korea. But, the Soviet depth of geography that renders power projection into the Soviet Heartland so impractical when guided by a scheme of conquest, also renders multiple-frontier defense very difficult or even militarily impractical for Moscow (against determined assault by first-class, or second-class allied to first-class, powers). Maritime power projection by Great Britain and France was logistically far superior to landpower projection by Imperial Russia in the Crimea, 1854–56.[2] In 1904–05, Imperial Russia was neither able nor willing to wage more than a distinctly limited war in Manchuria and Korea against Japan. Furthermore, notwithstanding the advances registered since 1904–05 in transportation technology, in the Russian/Soviet industrial base, and in relative Russian/Soviet military power compared with her potential enemies, it is plain beyond a reasonable doubt that the US-led maritime alliance could project military power more economically to and beyond the frontier of the Soviet Far East than could the Soviet Union itself.[3]

---

[1] A superb discussion is H.P. Willmott, *The Barrier and the Javelin: Japanese and Allied Pacific Strategies, February to June 1942* (Annapolis, MD: Naval Institute Press, 1983), particularly p. 44.

[2] Particularly in the context of allied naval demonstrations in the Baltic that denied Russia the option of concentrating on her problems in the South. In the words of C.E. Callwell, "Russia was striving in vain to meet the Allied army in the Crimea on equal terms, while all the time tens of thousands of her soldiers were lying idle near the Baltic shores, magnetized by the sea-power of the foe." *The Effect of Maritime Command on Land Campaigns since Waterloo* (Edinburgh: William Blackwood and Sons, 1897), pp. 181–82.

[3] In practice this might not be the case if, with a "swing" strategy, US maritime power were to accord the Atlantic and Indian Oceans higher priority than the Pacific. As in 1942, the US armed forces in a future global conflict are going to be confronted with more demands than they have ready resources—and strategy is about making choices. But, we are told on high authority and for excellent reasons that: "America's increasing commercial and energy interdependence with Asia, and the growth of the Soviet Pacific Fleet—now the largest of the four Soviet fleets—have negated the so-called 'swing strategy' of the 1960s and 1970s, which planned to reinforce the Atlantic Fleet with combatants from the Pacific in time of crisis. Today, the United States has an Asian orientation at least equal to its historic engagement in Europe." John F. Lehman, Jr., "The 600–Ship Navy," in Watkins et al., *The*

Location of national territory obviously is important, but so is distance. In terms of defense logistics in Eurasia, 1904–1905 has much to say to us today. The strategic meaning of geography has to be specific to political context. Soviet ability to project power from, or defend, its borders in Northern Europe, Southwest Asia, and Northeast Asia is not just an elementary matter for logistic calculation. What is the political-military context? If the Soviet Union is fighting, or anticipating having to fight, in Central, Southern, and Northern Europe, her ability to do more than hold her own — and probably not even that — in Northeast Asia, *inter alia,* must be in doubt.

Whatever one's judgment on the defense policy issues of the day, there are basic, enduring attributes of the United States as a distinctive security community that flow from geography. Strategic geography typically is Janus-like in its implications, as some of the points discussed below illustrate.

First, the United States is strategically insular. The military weakness of Canada and Mexico, effectively—though to a diminishing degree, given the disorder in Central America—renders the United States an island nation.[4]

Second, to be a military power of note, the United States, by reason of geography, has to rely on maritime capabilities. In the twenty-first century, as in both world wars, if the United States and her allies do not enjoy a "working" quality of sea control, then US garrisons cannot be supplied and relieved, and expeditionary forces cannot move or be supplied and reinforced (and, if need be, rescued so as to fight again). Changes in transportation technology between 1900 and, prospectively, 2000 will not alter the validity of the proposition that a sufficiency of freedom in American use of the sea is the *sine qua non* for any of the strategy designs of the leading contending schools of thought on US defense policy.

Third, because of the continental extent of its territory, the immigrant character of virtually all of its people, its liberal-idealist

---

[4] The outstanding discussion of this proposition and its implications remains Spykman, *America's Strategy in World Politics.* Also see Wilkinson, "Spykman and Geopolitics." *Maritime Strategy,* p. 22. Also relevant are Harlan K. Ullman, "The Pacific and US Naval Policy," *Naval Forces,* vol. VI (1985), pp. 36–45; and Eliot A. Cohen, "Do We Still Need Europe?" *Commentary,* vol. 81, no. 1 (January 1986), pp. 28–35.

philosophical tradition, and the blessings of geographical distance (absolute and psychological), the United States is not convincingly reconciled either to a prospectively permanent ''guardian'' role with respect to Rimland Eurasia, or to the use of the instruments of statecraft necessary for effective guardianship.[5] American insularity has bred powerful variants of isolationism/unilateralism across the political spectrum.[6]

Fourth, the specific course of American history has been influenced powerfully by geographical factors. American physical geography, in all its aspects, enabled political separation from the British Empire. The US geographical location enabled the British Royal Navy—sitting astride the chokepoints through which the naval power of any European state must transit—to protect the coasts of the United States as effectively as it did the coasts of Britain (that is, when the Royal Navy was well handled and, as a general if not absolute rule, when its continental-European enemies were distracted on land in Europe.) Geography has provided the economic sinews of American power, has influenced the attitudes and expectations of its people, and has influenced the selection of foreign allies and foes.

Fifth, the US insular strategic condition is either a strength or a weakness, depending upon relative US maritime power. The paradox is a familiar one. The US Navy could not, through decisive battle, attrition, or any variants thereof, defeat the Soviet Union strictly through action at sea, any more than the British Royal Navy could defeat *directly* the landpower of continental Imperial and later Nazi Germany. But, the US Navy would need to win its war— which, at minimum, would mean securing a working measure of sea control when and where the Western Alliance would require it —if the war in general were not to be lost. Should Soviet maritime power, of all kinds, succeed in practicing selectively a denial strategy on key sea lines of communication, then the West must either

---

[5] This, and related, points are developed in Colin S. Gray, ''American Strategic Culture and Military Performance,'' in Asa A. Clark IV, ed., *Defense Technology,* forthcoming. Also see the valuable discussion in Carnes Lord, ''American Strategic Culture,'' *Comparative Strategy,* vol. 5, no. 3 (1985), pp. 269–94.

[6] See Robert W. Tucker, ''Isolation and Intervention,'' *The National Interest,* no. 1 (Fall 1985), pp. 16–25.

lose or seek conflict resolution through desperately dangerous vertical nuclear escalation.

Sixth, geostrategically, the US security community is both blessed and cursed by the factor of distance. The loss-of-strength gradient with distance requires careful application to particular cases,[7] but it remains a general truth about transportation and logistics.[8] The oceanic distance surrounding North America that hinders overseas enemies, particularly when confronted with superior naval power, also is vastly costly for the projection of American power. Even with considerable host nation support, US forces in Europe must function as expeditionary forces. The need for airlift and sealift assets can be minimized, however, if one is prepared to select forward garrison locations for people and equipment. Leaving aside the issue of alliance political requirements, forward garrisons located and sized by what amounts to a political gridlock contribute to inflexibility in posture and policy; and garrisons located and sized as much, if not more, for political as for military reasons may have high costs in military terms. This is not to prejudge the running debate between self-styled continental/coalition strategists and maritime strategists, though it is to signal a view that the United States would have greater flexibility in global strategy were more of the heavy forward defense duties of NATO in Europe laid upon Europeans.

---

[7] As, for example, in Albert Wohlstetter, "Illusions of Distance," *Foreign Affairs,* vol. 46, no. 2 (January 1968), pp. 242–55.

[8] In the 1920s and 1930s both American and Japanese naval planners calculated that a fleet would lose approximtely 10% of its combat effectiveness for every 1,000 sea miles travelled from its base. Given that the home base of the US Pacific Fleet until 1940 was San Pedro, this was or should have been a depressing calculation with respect to the likelihood of near-term relief for a Philippines under Japanese siege. The attrition that tends to be wrought by sheer distance, terrain, and climate have been demonstrated by the fate of Napoleon's and Hitler's invasions of Russia. A respected British military historian has observed that "the part played by the Red Army in 1941 in halting the enemy advance has been exaggerated by Soviet historians. Success was due mainly to geography and climate, and thereafter to Stalin's determination." Albert Seaton, *The Russo-German War, 1941–45* (New York: Praeger, 1970), p. 221. See also Martin van Creveld, *Supplying War: Logistics from Wallenstein to Patton* (Cambridge: Cambridge University Press, 1977), Chapter 5. It may be worth recalling that Napoleon crossed the Niemen on June 23, 1812 with more than 400,000 men, but reached Moscow on September 15 with only 95,000. Clausewitz's participation in the 1812 debacle (while in Russia's service) undoubtedly influenced his theoretical writings on the diminishing power of the offensive (with distance) in war.

On the one hand, valid geopolitical generalities may be offered about the comparative US advantage in maritime power over the Soviet Union, such as ease of access to the open ocean, absence of land-frontier military distractions, and so forth. Similar plausible lectures may be delivered on the central geostrategic location of the maritime United States in terms of Rimland Eurasia. On the other hand, those valid generalities and plausible lectures have to be considered in the context both of the fact that the maritime alliance of the West faces a threat on one geographical axis of potential advance in particular, and of the proposition that that threat must be countered directly at virtually all costs. Specifically, it is fairly orthodox to maintain that peninsular NATO-Europe is the proximate (not ultimate, for Americans) prize in the Soviet-American struggle, that it faces a landpower threat of daunting proportions, and that there could be no imaginable compensation available elsewhere to the United States for the political loss of Western Europe to Soviet territorial control or hegemony.

GEOPOLITICS AND ALLIANCE: THE SEAPOWER VERSUS LANDPOWER OPPOSITION REVISITED

It is partially, though only partially, correct to consider the maritime power of the United States as the functional successor to the maritime power that Great Britain exercised, with specific benefit to the British view, as well as to the general benefit, of international order, from the late seventeenth century until the middle of the twentieth century.[9] British maritime power, a concept and a force traditionally held to be synonymous with British power,[10] consistently, if not always competently, was directed in an anti-hegemonic role. In the multipolar world of post-Westphalian (1648) Europe, an anti-hegemonic policy generally meant an anti-French policy, given that France, for reasons of demography and, after 1789, of energy of political system, was the country most threatening to the continental

---

[9] The best treatment of recent times is Paul M. Kennedy, *The Rise and Fall of British Naval Mastery* (New York: Scribner's, 1976).

[10] An idea propagated assiduously, successfully, and with some good reasons by Alfred T. Mahan. For a recent assessment, see Philip A. Crowl, "Alfred Thayer Mahan: The Naval Historian," in Peter Paret, ed., *Makers of Modern Strategy: from Machiavelli to the Nuclear Age* (Princeton, NJ: Princeton University Press, 1986), Chapter 16.

balance of power. The First (1905) and Second (1911) Morocco (Agadir) Crises respectively registered publicly, and underlined the extent to which, British threat identification had altered from the traditional to a new enemy, Imperial Germany.

From the sixteenth century, when she was only a minor offshore power, to the mid-twentieth, when she was advanced in her *relative* economic decline, Great Britain sought to deny success to territorial or hegemonic imperialism on the part of any continental country or coalition — a policy, or really precept of statecraft, that required considerable diplomatic agility. The same rationale that for four hundred years moved British statesmen to join or organize coalitions to deny continental hegemony, has been the publicly underacknowledged geopolitical *Leitmotiv* for American international security policy since 1917 (though with an extensive lapse in the interwar period). A continental super-state would be able, if unopposed by land, to translate superior landpower into what might become superior seapower. This was why Britain fought in World War I. A Germany victorious on land would be at liberty to generate the material basis for victory at sea.

From a geopolitical perspective, the Soviet challenge to American security is the same as was the German. Notwithstanding the more obvious differences between the Third Reich and the USSR, both have sought — and, in the case of the latter, is still seeking —political preponderance in Eurasia.[11] Just as Britain could not be an agile balancer of power in twentieth century European diplomacy, so the United States is required to oppose, indeed to organize and lead opposition to, the Soviet drive for hegemony if that drive is to be contained or reversed.

At this juncture it is important to recognize the somewhat changing geopolitical significance of nuclear weapons for American security over the past forty years and, by logical extension, to the end of the century. From the end of World War II until the mid-1960s, nuclear weapons served persuasively—both in contemporary analysis and in retrospect—as an effective equalizer, or more than an equalizer, for the maritime alliance of the West to organize and hold a forward containing line.[12] The "extended deterrent" repre-

[11] This is not to argue that Soviet political and military leaders are disciples of Halford Mackinder or any other Western geopolitical theorists. See Peter H. Vigor, "The Soviet View of Geopolitics," in Zoppo and Zorgbibe, eds., *On Geopolitics,* pp. 131–39.

[12] See David Alan Rosenberg, "The Origins of Overkill: Nuclear Weapons and American Strategy, 1945–1960," *International Security,* vol. 7, no. 4 (Spring 1983), pp. 3–71.

sented by the US nuclear arsenal was *the* security guarantor for
Rimland Eurasia against Soviet conquest and/or hegemony. British,
and later American, seapower historically had been effective in
laying siege to continental landpower only in so far as the enemy
was seriously engaged on land. The Anglo-American air and maritime threat to Hitler's *Festung Europa* proved to be decisive while
most of Germany's military strength was inextricably detained and
attrited elsewhere.[13]

The Western problem after World War II, once the US expeditionary forces had been demobilized, was that there was no
near-term available, or even prospective, Eurasian distractor of Soviet military effort. In the form of atomic weapons, historical good
fortune provided the United States and its economically-exhausted
European clients with what appeared to be a relatively (relative to
conventionally armed forces, that is) inexpensive and very credible
means of containing further realization of Soviet hegemonic am-
bitions in Europe. In effect, nuclear weapons assumed the role for
the offshore power formerly filled by militarily strong continental
allies. The strategic rationale for "The Great Deterrent" functioning
as an "extended deterrent" was eminently reasonable while the
United States enjoyed what is very loosely termed strategic superiority, and which might better be described as major military advantage.[14] In the jargon of modern strategic theory, the United States

---

[13] Soviet historians have a way of neglecting to notice that Anglo-American seapower saved
the Soviet Union. By an authoritative contemporary German estimate, in the Fall of 1943
the German Army deployed 2,440,000 men in the West, as compared with 2,800,000 in
Russia, which—even allowing for the restricted "garrison" quality of many of the former
—is an impressive figure. Of greater moment was the fact that by the spring of 1944 as
many as 42 percent of the *field divisions* of the German Army were deployed in Western
Europe and the Mediterranean, fighting in Italy, or tied down by the ubiquitous menace
posed by Anglo-American seapower. Seaton, *The Russo-German War, 1941–45*, pp. 396,
590. Anyone still skeptical over the contribution of Anglo-American seapower to the Soviet
victory should recognize that US food supply, by and large, fed the Soviet Army in the later
stages of the war, and that Soviet military holdings of motor vehicles totalled 665,000 in
May 1945—of which 427,000 had been supplied by the United States and Britain (Ibid.,
p. 589). The motorization of the 60 divisions of the Soviet High Command reserve (in
particular) was critical to the combat performance of the Soviet Army. Delivery of the vital
food and motor vehicles was possible only because of Anglo-American command of the sea.
[14] See Edward N. Luttwak, "The Problems of Extending Deterence," in *The Future of
Strategic Deterrence, Part 1*, Adelphi Papers no. 160 (London: IISS, Autumn 1980), pp.
31–7; Anthony H. Cordesman, *Deterrence in the 1980s, Part 1: American Strategic Forces
and Extended Deterrence*, Adelphi Papers no. 175 (London: IISS, Summer 1982); and Walter
B. Slocombe, "Extended Deterrence."

could extend nuclear deterrence so as to cover the territories of some distant allies because it had, or was believed to have, vertical "escalation dominance."

In Soviet geostrategic perspective, from the late 1940s until the early-to-mid 1960s, a NATO-Europe vulnerable to invasion was hostage to moderation in US strategic behavior. Until the Soviet Union acquired a secure second-strike capability against the United States in the mid-1960s, US freedom of direct military action against the Soviet homeland was offset by the damage that Soviet armies could do to vital US interests in peninsular Europe. In the American perspective, unmatched US strategic nuclear prowess offset the local gross imbalance in conventional-force capabilities. US strategic nuclear superiority, translated into anticipation in the East and the West that the United States would enjoy escalation dominance in any trial by combat, meant that US risks and US interests were tolerably in balance with respect to the security implications of alliance ties.

The rout of American isolationism by Franklin Roosevelt, critically assisted by the abysmal statecraft of Japan and Germany, was confirmed by the Truman Doctrine of 1947, reconfirmed by the outcome of the great debate over the NATO Treaty in 1949, and was set in concrete with the activation of SHAPE in 1951 in the immediate aftermath of the Korean shock. "Atlanticism" in the 1950s and through much of the 1960s could refer to the fact that the denial of Soviet hegemony over Western Europe was a vital interest of the United States — after all, the United States already had fought two wars within living memory for the geopolitical purpose of thwarting hegemonism in Europe — and that it would be in the self-interest of the United States actually to wage as much war as might prove necessary in order to protect that interest. "Escalation dominance" refers to the ability to prosecute deliberately a war at higher and higher levels of violence in reasonable expectation of securing an improved political outcome. US strategic superiority, though admittedly more and more dependent upon the securing of a favorable operational context, meant that the United States was not risking the literal survival of American society with the strategic nuclear threat it posed to the USSR in support of NATO-Europe.

Since the late 1950s, the value, on most figures of relative merit, of the United States' geographically forward-located security clients, particularly in East Asia, has greatly increased. Whereas the buffer zone of the Soviet homeland in Europe comprises unreliable and relatively poor satellites,[15] the United States has a coterie of security clients who are presumably reliable and generally economically successful allies. However, Soviet achievements in competitive armament of all kinds since the early 1960s have wrought an unacknowledged, or certainly an underacknowledged, apparent revolution in the relationship between risk and interest of the United States' formal security connection with Western Europe.

The US interest in denying the Soviet Union territorial control or hegemony over Western Europe is objectively less today than it was in the 1950s or 1960s.[16] Soviet *contrôle* of Western Europe effectively would help resolve some of the economic problems of the Soviet Union, but it would likely render others more intractable.[17] More or less rigorous integration of Western and Eastern European economies, with terms of trade highly advantageous to Moscow, and within a new security framework provided by the European-wide applicability of the Brezhnev Doctrine, would be a dramatic and possibly irreversible development in the balance of world power. This is not to deny either that Soviet direction of a European-wide economy would affect very adversely the produc-

---

[15] Not to mention possibly mutinous satellites. See Stephen Peter Rosen, ''Mutiny and the Warsaw Pact,'' *The National Interest*. no. 2 (Winter 1985/6), pp. 74–82.

[16] Europe is, of course, still very important in the world economy (with 17.3% of the gross world product) and to the United States, but it is not economically more important than the countries of the Asian rim. The issue of the relative economic and strategic importance of Europe to the United States, and why it has declined and seems destined to continue to decline, is well handled in Cohen, ''Do We Still Need Europe,'' particularly pp. 29–30.

[17] For an obvious example, the granaries of the world lie in the Americas and Australia. Using the time-honored, if slow working, instrument of maritime blockade, a United States excluded—forcibly or otherwise—from Europe could give the leaders of a hegemonic Soviet Union the same problems that ultimately brought down Imperial Germany. In the words of the British official history: ''The outstanding feature of the situation was this: that the Allies were, and the Central Powers were not able, if necessary, to continue the war for another year.'' C. Ernest Fayle, *History of the Great War: Seaborne Trade, Vol. II, The Period of Unrestricted Submarine Warfare* (London: John Murray, 1924), pp. 411–12. For World War II, see the superb study by W.N. Medlicott, *History of the Second World War (United Kingdom Civil Series): The Economic Blockade*, two volumes (London: H.M.S.O., 1952 and 1959).

tivity of Western European economic assets, or that the process of executing a controlling influence would not bring with it new security problems for the Soviet Union — not the least of which would be the unresolved German Problem. The "quality of interest" case for US security commitments to NATO-Europe has diminished in persuasiveness since 1949 relative to commitments to East Asia, but remains nonetheless very high indeed.[18]

What has altered since 1949, and even more dramatically since the mid-1960s, is the quality of risk for the United States that is attached to the NATO commitment — at least for so long as the structure of NATO's military strategy remains unaltered in its essentials. Over the course of the past twenty years the Soviet Union has constructed a comprehensive, multi-level nuclear counterdeterrent that has negated the prospective effectiveness of the very architecture of NATO strategy. Flexible response is good enough while Soviet leaders lack a truly powerful political incentive to consider very seriously a military solution to a close-to-intolerable political problem. The fact that in political and military logic NATO's strategy no longer should "work"—because its objective basis in the terms of the East-West military relationship has eroded catastrophically—cannot serve to remove the objective risk for the Soviet Union that NATO countries, and particularly the United States, might offer.[19] Soviet students of US and NATO strategy debates can hardly have failed to notice the prominence accorded uncertainty, elevated to the status of a principle of deterrence, and the bizarre concepts of "risks that leave something to chance" and of the "rationality of irrationality."[20]

In American perspective, strictly speaking, denial of Soviet hegemony over Western Europe is an interest well worth fighting for, but it is not an interest of direct and immediate survival value for American society. Given that proportionality is an important principle for the guidance of statecraft, the quantity of sacrifice the

---

[18] An outstanding recent treatment of US national interests is Donald E. Nuechterlein, *America Overcommitted: United States National Interests in the 1980s* (Lexington, KY: University Press of Kentucky, 1985).

[19] See Robert Jervis, *The Illogic of American Nuclear Strategy* (Ithaca, NY: Cornell University Press, 1984).

[20] Lawrence Freedman's widely praised book, *The Evolution of Nuclear Strategy* (London: Macmillan, 1981), effectively gives up on nuclear strategy *as strategy*.

United States should be prepared to make in defense of an interest ought to be proportional to the "worth" of that interest. The Soviet military modernization program has raised the possible price of alliance to an intolerable level for the United States. This is the core of the strategic logic of neo-isolationism. The banner carriers for "America First" in the 1980s include commentator-theorists of both liberal and conservative political persuasions. When stated rigorously and honestly, neo-isolationism as a prescription for US foreign policy does not rest upon the proposition that the United States should be indifferent to international order beyond the Americas; rather, it claims that a self-regarding prudence of the most basic kind — a concern for the physical safety of Americans — suggests strongly that foreign security entanglements, on balance, contribute to American insecurity in the nuclear age. In the words of probably the most articulate analyst of neo-isolationism, Robert W. Tucker:

> The chief attraction of a policy of withdrawal to this hemisphere is that it would avoid the principal risk a policy of global involvement, with or without alliances, must incur. It would avoid the risk of war and, above all, nuclear war . . . . nuclear missile weapons give substance to the long-discredited isolationist dream. So long as it is clear that they will be employed only in the direct defense of the homeland, they confer a physical security that is virtually complete, and that the loss of allies cannot alter. Instead, alliances must *detract* from physical security, since it is the prospect of defending allies that may one day result in a war destructive of this security.[21] (Emphasis in the original.)

The neo-isolationist critique of US postwar security policy is a powerful one, provided the geopolitical and defense-analytical reasoning upon which it rests is well founded. There can be little doubt that most of the possible powder trails to a nuclear war that might engulf the US homeland lead from peripheral Eurasia. It is the US determination to deny Soviet hegemony over the Rimlands of Eurasia that, in one perspective at least, provides the fuel for conflict and even for nuclear conflagration. It is essential to identify both the key assumptions or, in more competent and honest analyses,

---

[21] Robert W. Tucker, "Containment and the Search for Alternatives: A Critique," in Aaron Wildavsky, ed., *Beyond Containment: Alternative American Policies Toward the Soviet Union* (San Francisco: Institute for Contemporary Studies Press, 1983), pp. 81–82.

acknowledged hopes, that underpin the core of neo-isolationist arguments, and the fallacies in those arguments. Key assumptions include the following:

1. A belief that the Soviet Union either would not desire to, or could not, pursue its quest for hegemony beyond Eurasia.

2. A belief that, whatever Soviet doctrine may say or be held to imply, in practice a Soviet Union left by US withdrawal as the security organizer, or guardian, for Eurasia, would be content with the new *de facto* definition of hemispheric spheres of influence. The Western Hemisphere of the Americas and possibly Oceania (the South-West Pacific) would be conceded, of practical geostrategic necessity, to the US security system.

3. A belief that for many decades to come, at the least, the Soviet Union would be so heavily engaged in ordering its newly expanded imperium that a political condition akin to a condominium would prevail in superpower relations.

4. A hope that the United States, through wise management of the timing and manner of its security withdrawal, would not leave a vacuum of countervailing power, an unlocked door that the Soviet Union could push open with minimal need to resort to explicit threats.

5. A hope that the change in the Soviet security condition effected by the US security withdrawal, and the impact on the Soviet political system and culture of (possible/probable) acquisition of new security clients with very different political and social traditions, would have—cumulatively—a benign impact upon the character and purposes of Soviet power.

6. A belief that even if peninsular Europe could not resist some variant of "Finlandization," and even if the Soviet state were able to translate the extension of its geographical security perimeter into much greater strength for the further prosecution of an inalienable bid for global hegemony, oceanic distance and an American defense postural focus upon maritime power and strategic forces (nuclear and non-nuclear) must prospectively forever deny the Soviet Union the ability to lay siege successfully to North America.

There is sufficient truth or plausibility in the above points that, looking to the next century, the generic neo-isolationist challenge to the now forty-five year long Atlanticist tradition of collective security is a serious one. In the historical sweep of the American experience, it remains to be seen whether the interventionism of 1941 to the present day is an aberration or, generically if not in geostrategic detail, is permanent.

More or less "splendid isolation" should not be confused with unilateralism, though the two, in practice, may amount to much the same. Insular strategic geography, until the advent of truly inter-continental airpower and missile power in the 1950s (for the United States), permitted a voluntarism, a freedom for unilateral decision to commit or not to commit, that geographical contiguity of threat has not allowed to Eurasian continental states. Even in the missile age, it can be argued that nuclear weapons function quite strictly as counterdeterrents, thereby failing, prospectively, to effect a rev-olution in the likely timescale (and geographical scope) of war.[22] Just as British "blue water" theorists and practitioners for four hundred years forged a unilateralist tradition in strategy[23]—though most definitely not an isolationist tradition—exploiting the inherent flexibility in seapower and the then superior mobility of seapower over landpower (as a general, though not universal, rule), so there is an analogous American school of thought today.

The United States, with her geostrategic long-suit of central maritime position between Asia and Europe-Africa, given the global character of her security concerns, and given the inherent vulner-abilities of a Soviet defense perimeter so extensive (and so sub-stantially flanked by a major, if second-class, enemy in China) that it invites threats on multiple axes, cannot help but be interested in avoiding so heavy a specific forward defense commitment that many of her geostrategic advantages effectively would be foresworn. The dilemma is a familiar one. In World War I, Britain had to make an

[22] This sentence begs a host of questions, the detailed discussion of which far exceeds the scope of this enquiry. The point is that both of the rival alliance systems and superpowers have massive incentives not to have resort to nuclear weapons, save perhaps in the direst of strategic emergencies. See Colin S. Gray, "Global Protracted War: Conduct and Termina-tion," in Stephen Cimbala, ed., *Strategic War Termination* (New York: Praeger, 1986).
[23] The question of just how much freedom of action British statesmen really enjoyed in the nineteenth century is probed rigorously in Christopher Howard, *Britain and the Casus Belli, 1822–1902: A study of Britain's international position from Canning to Salisbury* (London: Athlone Press, 1974).

enormous continental landpower commitment to the defense of France, because defeat on the Western Front could have meant general defeat in the war. The scale of the British commitment to France was so great, however, that potentially very important efforts on the flanks of the Central Powers (e.g., Gallipoli in 1915) were conducted too late with too little. The United States today and through the end of the century has to decide where to strike the balance between the allocation of scarce resources to aid in the defense of the vital center, that is to say NATO's Central Front, and the allocation of assets in a reserve function for flexible exploitation of Washington's comparative (maritime) geostrategic advantages.

By far the most important fact about the structure of the US security condition for the next several decades, and almost certainly for much longer than that, pertains to the basic character of the Soviet-American antagonism. One cannot frame geostrategic propositions soundly in the absence of a clear understanding of the foundations of that antagonism. Such understanding has to provide the framework within which scenarios are generated and in the light of which strategic policy advice must be assessed.

For reasons both Soviet and Russian, the Soviet Union's quarrel with the United States is with the US existence as the only country capable of organizing and executing effective resistance to the expansion of Soviet hegemony. The Soviet Union may or may not be an historically typical great power; it really does not matter, because the great powers of balance-of-power Europe were restrained in the scope of their ambition by the countervailing endeavors of the other great powers. The basis for US hostility to the Soviet Union, today or in 2000, lies both in the nature of the Soviet system as an actor in world politics — with the motives for outward pressure endemic in the domestic stability requirements of that system — and in the bipolar structure of the contemporary international security system. The Soviet Union is the enemy of the United States because of capabilities of all kinds, actual and potential. Soviet-American antagonism superficially will be to a degree specific to time and place, but the superpower quarrel is not "about" Berlin, relative influence in Beijing, or any other geostrategic particular. Soviet power is self-justifying and has no formal geostrategic bounds to its ambition short of achievement of a physically-impractical global empire. There is much to recommend the following argument advanced by Robert V. Daniels:

> Americans must face a basic fact: Russia is a mammoth power that will not disappear or cease to challenge the United States, regardless of the colorations of its government. The contest for world influence between the United States and Russia is grounded in history —indeed it was foreseen by writers in Europe and American more than a century ago. Russia will continue to be guided by the pride, ambitions, and interests that have carried over from prerevolutionary times—and no mere alteration in regime or ideology will quickly eliminate them.[24]

Recognition of the systemic character of bipolar superpower conflict does not carry necessary, specific implications for US military strategy and force structure. However, decisions on strategy and posture are unlikely to be correct if the character of the conflict is not assessed accurately. It would be difficult to improve upon Clausewitz' statement that:

> The first, the supreme, the most far-reaching act of judgment that the statesman and commander have to make is to establish . . . the kind of war on which they are embarking: neither mistaking it for, nor trying to turn it into, something that is alien to its nature.[25]

The United States could have chosen to wage only a limited war of strategic position against Japan in 1942. For very understandable reasons, the United States elected to wage total war—it was Japanese statesmen who misunderstood the nature of the war that they had unleashed. The war in peace that is Soviet-American security relations fits by analogy neither US nor Japanese intentions in 1941–42. Soviet intentions, unlike Japanese, are not geographically bounded, while the military expression of those intentions does not lend itself to definitive overthrow in some variant of decisive battle or campaign. Pending the possible maturing and heavy, multi-tiered deployment of US strategic defense technologies, the

---

[24] Robert V. Daniels, *Russia: The Roots of Confrontation* (Cambridge, MA: Harvard University Press, 1985), p. 358.
[25] Carl von Clausewitz, *On War* (Michael Howard and Peter Paret, eds.) (Princeton, NJ: Princeton University Press, 1976), p. 88.

armed forces no longer can function in a literal sense as the shield of the Republic.

The United States is at considerable liberty today, looking out towards the next century, to decide where and how it will oppose Soviet hegemonism, but it is not at liberty to withdraw from what has to be a condition of opposition. The central fallacy of neo-isolationism is the general proposition that the United States can enhance its security by withdrawing from those foreign security commitments that, purportedly, give offense in Soviet eyes. The fallacy lies in the belief that it is the geostrategic detail of the US guardianship role that is provocative in Moscow. Soviet hostility towards the United States will contine until either the Soviet state is transformed, by whatever mix of cumulatively irresistible pressures, or the structure of the world balance of power is altered.

A Soviet Union essentially left in charge of security in Eurasia will not have attained thereby any facsimile of a natural security perimeter — notwithstanding the landpower focus of Soviet strategic culture.[26] US statesmen, thinking that they should not risk American survival in defense of interests of less than survival quality,[27] would find that they would have shifted the geographical terms of super-power competition, inevitably, towards contention over assets closer to survival quality than had been judged to be the case with respect to Rimland Eurasia.

In the 1980s, the Soviet Union, one may be sure, regards her friends and allies of convenience in the Caribbean and Central America as a useful and highly expendable diversion for limited US policy energy. However, in the event of a comprehensive US security withdrawal from Eurasia, Soviet statecraft should be expected to begin in earnest to lay siege to the American homeland. Theorists of international relations differ over the probability of major shifts in the balance of power promoting yet greater shifts in the same direction, as "fence sitting" states elect to join a bandwagon in fear that, if they do not, that bandwagon may roll over them. A no-less-

[26] The concept of strategic culture is explored in: Jack L. Snyder, *The Soviet Strategic Culture: Implications for Limited Nuclear Operations*, R-2154–AF (Santa Monica, CA: RAND, September 1977); Gray, *Nuclear Strategy and National Style;* and Gray, *Geopolitics, Strategic Culture, and National Security,* forthcoming.

[27] A rigorous discussion of criteria for identifying *survival,* as opposed to vital, interests, is provided in Nuechterlein, *America Overcommitted,* particularly pp. 10–11.

popular view holds that an imbalance in power tends to be self-correcting, as successful aggrandizement triggers the opposition that must arrest its progress.[28] In an extreme form, this argument holds that should the United States decide no longer to lead an intercontinental Western Alliance, but rather to laager its wagons (or carrier task forces) around the Western Hemisphere, Soviet efforts to exploit this historical development inexorably would cause such security alarms in Western Europe, China, and Japan, that the politically impossible would then be possible. In this hopeful view, a European Defense Community would be forged in tacit coalition with a Sino-Japanese alliance or, at the least, an *entente trés cordiale*.

As a Panglossian vision, this happy prospect has everything to recommend it. Unfortunately, responsible US planners in the 1980s and 1990s can have no confidence that the United States in fact would be able to pass the security organizer's baton to the leaders of new architectures for collective defense in Europe and Asia. There can be little doubt that the continuation of a US definition of its security perimeter as lying on-shore in Rimland Eurasia, from Kirkenes to Seoul, does serve effectively to discourage local defense initiatives. Still, it is a great leap of political faith to proceed from recognition of major incentives for Eurasia Rimland countries to take suitable charge of their own regional security interests, to belief that such creativity and determination actually would occur in a timely fashion.

It is beyond the mandate of this discussion to design ways in which the United States might explore in some safety the devolution of some current Eurasian security duties upon successor security regimes, consistent with the protection of US vital interests. For the purposes of this enquiry, what matters is recognition that the United States cannot remove itself from the status of Soviet "public enemy number one" by means of redrawing the geographical perimeter of US vital interests. Actual and potential US capabilities define the US role as principal threat in Soviet calculation.[29] For ideological

[28] An optimistic thesis that finds favor with Stephen M. Walt, "Alliance Formation and the Balance of World Power," *International Security*, vol. 9, no. 4 (Spring 1985), pp. 3–41.

[29] In addition, Soviet ideology specifies an existential connection between "imperialism" (the final stage of capitalism) and the danger of war. For the benefit of a credulous Western audience, Soviet leaders talk as if the details of US defense policy are important for stability (a very Western, and particularly American, concept) and peace, but their system of beliefs

and *Realpolitik* motives, the Soviet Union will never voluntarily permit the United States a quiet retirement from the perils of nuclear-age power politics, wherein "life, liberty, and the pursuit of happiness" can be pursued by a country determinedly inoffensive to Soviet interests in world affairs. It is not the Soviet way in prudent statecraft to place reliance upon voluntary self-restraint on the part of others, if the more certain result of physical incapacitation is available.

There is much to recommend a geopolitical perspective upon the superpower antagonism which argues that, in Soviet eyes, the proximate American offense is its preservation of a large, prosperous, and well-armed bridgehead in NATO-Europe. Security and stability in Soviet politicial and strategic culture flows from Soviet preponderance. Pluralism in security frameworks is as alien to Soviet state wishes as it would be in the domestic political system of the Soviet imperium. However, the geopolitical referents of Soviet-American competition are not confined as by some law of geopolitics to US security bridgeheads in Europe and Asia. Since the tide of battle turned definitively in World War II with the failure of the last great German offensive in the East (Kursk) in July 1943, the Soviet Union has secured the Eurasian Heartland, has moved from the status of a regional great power, to being *the* regional great power, to being the second-class superpower, to being a still-candidate first-class, which is to say global, superpower. To be a truly global superpower, however the Soviet Union must transcend its still substantially landlocked condition and break convincingly out of the Heartland.[30]

While the United States has enormous positional and logistical advantages over the Soviet Union *vis à vis* potential conflict in the Western Hemisphere and its maritime approaches, the strategic value of geography can alter dramatically with political, as well as technological, circumstances. The disadvantages under which the US Navy would labor in seeking to exercise sea control or to project power in waters very close to the Soviet homeland are too obvious to be worth citing. However, critics of extant US foreign security

---

identifies the risk of war with the political character and dynamics of societies and social change.

[30] This thesis is developed in Gray, *The Geopolitics of the Nuclear Era.*

entanglements are wont to appear to forget, or at least to neglect, the no-less-obvious contemporary advantages enjoyed by the US Navy. Those advantages include a "chokepoint" control denying Soviet forces access to the open ocean that is scarcely less impressive than that exercised by the British Royal Navy in its heyday.[31] The surface navy of Imperial Germany could not effect a sortie onto the sea lines of communication of the Western allies, save through the unacceptable tactic of offering itself up to a very strong probability of total destruction in a decisive battle in the North Sea. Without denying the survival risk to the United States that is inherent in leading opposition to Soviet hegemonic policies in Eurasia, the fact remains that forward-located allies and friends of the United States, in negative terms, are denying Moscow access to geography critical for Soviet global power projection. The Allies provide large naval, land, and airpower barriers to Soviet access to the oceanic approaches to the Americas. On the positive side, the Eurasian allies of the United States provide a forward geostrategic basis for US access to the Soviet imperium.

Neo-isolationists, and even unilateralists who tend to disparage the security value to the United States of the NATO alliance as currently organized in its security arrangements, need to recognize some geopolitical considerations of enduring relevance for the very structure of American security. First, the beginning of wisdom is recognition of the validity of Nicholas Spykman's 1944 dictum that the United States'

> . . . main political objective, both in peace and in war, must therefore be to prevent the unification of the Old World centers of power in a coalition hostile to her own interests.[32]

Spykman simply is repeating for the United States what had been the overriding operating principle for British statecraft since the time of Henry VIII.

Second, the greatest of twentieth-century geopolitical theorists,

---

[31] "5 keys lock up the world! Singapore, the Cape, Alexandria, Gibraltar, Dover. These five keys belong to England, and the five great Fleets of England . . . will hold these keys!" Sir John Fisher, quoted in Arthur Marder, *The Anatomy of British Sea Power: A History of British Naval Policy in the Pre-Dreadnought Era, 1880–1905* (Hamden, CT: Archon Books, 1964; first pub. 1940), p. 473.
[32] Spykman, *The Geography of the Peace*, p. 45.

Sir Halford Mackinder, recognized as early as 1943 that this time, predicting Soviet power in the future, the wolf truly would be at the Western door:

> All things considered, the conclusion is unavoidable that if the Soviet Union emerges from this war as conqueror of Germany, she must rank as the greatest land power on the globe. Moreover, she will be the power in the strategically strongest defensive position. The Heartland is the greatest natural fortress on earth. For the first time in history, it is manned by a garrison sufficient both in number and quality.[33]

Mackinder did not know about the Manhattan Project and— one should note — his conception of a Heartland to the "World Island" (the dual continent of Europe-Asia) originally was presented in 1904, before the realization of heavier-than-air flight. Nonetheless, this brief passage of 1943 vintage points directly to the third enduring truth of geopolitics relevant to US security. Preponderant landpower, if substantially uncontested and distracted by continental enemies still in the field, may be the basis from which superior seapower is developed and exercised.

If the United States politically, and as a consequence militarily, were expelled, or chose to withdraw, from European and Asian security entanglements, there would be a very severe danger that the "sources of seapower"[34] of Rimland Eurasia would not only be denied application to the pursuit of purposes congruent with US interests, but might be enlisted for participation in a new phase of Soviet *Weltpolitik*. Nuclear-armed, the United States should be secure against invasion, but a Soviet Union conceded preponderance in Eurasia would have the positional (geostrategic), economic, and the military bases for initiating a very serious challenge to the United States in the Americas. Soviet surface and sub-surface fleets no longer "locked up" or blockaded in the Arctic, the Baltic, the Black Sea, the Sea of Japan, and the Sea of Okhotsk, would not fear being in a crisis status of hostages upon the high seas, nor in time of war

---

[33] Mackinder, *Democratic Ideals and Reality*, pp. 272–73. An above average, useful intellectual biography is W.H. Parker, *Mackinder: Geography as an aid to statecraft* (Oxford: Clarendon Press, 1982).

[34] See Geoffrey Till et al., *Maritime Strategy and the Nuclear Age* (London: Macmillan, 1982), Chapter 3.

compelled to behave as fugitives if sailing outside the Soviet Union's erstwhile coastal sea bastions.

Overall, it cannot be doubted that the European and Asian allies of the United States, to greater and lesser degree, expend proportionately fewer national resources upon a supposedly common security enterprise than does the United States.[35] Furthermore, these Rimland allies constitute a geographically fractured chain of relatively exposed outposts (or US bridgeheads, in the Soviet view), commitment to the forward defense of which reduces very greatly the flexibility with which American policymakers might otherwise choose to direct the application of military power. NATO's Central Front, covering absolutely essential assets, simply would have to be defended with the utmost determination.

Soviet strategic planners, while hoping—though probably not expecting—to achieve a *Blitzkrieg* victory on the Central Front, might suspect that in the event of failure to secure a rapid and fatal rupture of NATO's linear, hard-crust defense, they could impose a theater-wide "Verdun" upon their enemies. In other words, Soviet planners probably expect that NATO would expend all available effort to attempt to hold the Central Front; this would not be a battle, or campaign, that NATO could afford to concede in order to fight again another day on more advantageous ground.[36]

The Soviet military experience in World War II was of a broad-front attritional struggle against a materially inferior enemy who was massively distracted by the need to garrison virtually the whole of Southern, Western, and Northern Europe, eventually to defend Italy and France against invasion, and to employ more than 65%

---

[35] American complaints concerning NATO-European under-spending on defense need to take account of the social and economic costs of conscription, of the allies' (involuntary) contribution of the potential battlefield, and of those US defense efforts that are specific to a global superpower. See Klaus Knorr, "Burden-Sharing in NATO: Aspects of US Policy," *Orbis*, vol. 29, no. 3 (Fall 1985), pp. 517–36.

[36] The German Chief of the General Staff, Erich von Falkenhayn, selected Verdun for the site of the first great German offensive in the West since the failure at Ypres in October–November 1914, precisely because its mix of military and political-symbolic value was calculated—correctly—to leave the French with no choice but to accept battle on terms chosen by the attacker. See C.R.M.F. Cruttwell, *A History of the Great War, 1914–1918* (Oxford: Clarendon Press, 1934), Chapter 15. In practice, predictably, German prestige came to be as heavily invested in the Verdun campaign as was French. Verdun did contribute towards the potential ruin of the French Army, as intended, but it contributed scarcely less to the ultimate ruin of the German Army.

of its air force in homeland defense. Soviet political and military leaders, prudentially recognizing that war is an uncertain business, have to be aware of the possibility that in the event of the failure of a short-war *Blitzkrieg,* they might then be confronted with the dilemma of either initiating nuclear escalation in an endeavor to snatch victory out of stalemate, or accepting a protracted ground war of attrition in Europe with a global enemy. In the course of the protracted war of attrition in Europe, the enemy economies that would be conducting crash-scale military mobilization would not resemble the Axis powers of 1941–45, but instead would be the world's economic leaders. Soviet strategic culture may have some difficulty believing that the Soviet Union could lose a prolonged, wholly (or very largely) conventional war, but the dominant Soviet military experience was of a one-front war against an underequipped and poorly commanded Germany. The differences with a putative World War III should be awesome, and profoundly deterring, in the Soviet perspective. Whether or not the maritime alliance of the West acts so as to provide itself with the strategy, the ready military means, and the defense-economic (including very high-technology) mobilization plans that would make a reality of the possible Soviet anxieties sketched here, must be a matter for conjecture at the present time.

US military commitments to an interrupted on-shore perimeter, from the North Cape of Norway to Eastern Turkey, risk the US ability to ''roll with the punch'' and recover, because too great a percentage of US deployed and readily mobilizable military power might be lost in the first battles. Given the advantages of the initiative for Soviet arms,[37] in the context both of very considerable initial numerical ground-force superiority and in ease of rapid reinforcement, it is all too obvious why the forward defense commitment to NATO-Europe could place the US homeland at survival risk after the passage of only a few days of theater combat.

However, Americans critical of NATO-European efforts for the common defense, and understandably worried lest there is today a foolish asymmetry between the quality of US risks and the quality of US interests in Europe, should remember that the allies of the

---

[37] And the advantages that the initiative grants for the employment of surprise and deception. See C.J. Dick, ''Catching NATO Unawares: Soviet Army surprise and deception techniques,'' *International Defense Review,* vol. 19, no. 1 (1986), pp. 21–26.

United States are contributing their national territories as potential battlefields for the forward, outpost defense of the Americas. Furthermore, it should be understood that a redefinition of the US defense perimeter would simply alter the geographical locale for agonizing decisions; it would not permit the United States to evade the harder problems associated with maintaining its security in the shadow of nuclear threats. So great would be the perils of a drastic scale of withdrawal of US security guarantees — from a known containing line to what? — and so much is it to the US advantage to keep the Soviet Union essentially landlocked, that there is everything to be said in favor of exploring rigorously how national US and allied military strategy (or strategies) can be improved so as better to balance ends and means. There is no compelling case for the United States to begin dismantling the geopolitical architecture of the maritime alliance of the West. Readers should ask themselves the following question: if the United States flinches from the prospect of nuclear escalation in defense of Norway, West Germany, or Turkey, what risks would be run ''for'' the Azores, Venezuela, or Panama?

3

GEOPOLITICS

CLEARING THE DECKS

The humorous though pointed quotation from Admiral Sir John
Jervis (Lord St. Vincent) with which this monograph began can
serve a useful purpose for this discussion. Sir John, with his ironic
caveat, (''I do not say the Frenchman will not come . . .''), was
underlining the absolute quality of security against invasion enjoyed
by a nation whose navy commanded the seas. If the irony in the
caveat is ignored as no longer appropriate, and the name of the
identified enemy is altered, Sir John's statement fits as the tersest
of summaries of the role of the US Navy. Suitably expanded, the
statement acknowledges what should be obvious—that naval power
alone cannot prevent the defeat of the United States and her allies.
The statement does claim, by plain implication, that naval power
of suitable quantity and quality and intelligently used, can prevent
the defeat of the United States and/or its allies by the enemy's
exercise of its naval power. Given the key role of sea lines of
communication as the interior lines of the maritime alliance of the
West, this is no small matter.

The Soviet Union could lose in the maritime dimension of a
major war, yet still win so definitively on land in Europe that it
would be able to rebuild its seapower so as to pose a maritime threat
to the Americas that, apart from the early decades of the Republic,
would be historically unprecedented. Recent debates in the United
States over different variants of maritime and coalition strategy have
not served the cause of balanced public understanding. Under pres-

sure to advocate effectively, rival theorists have erected convenient "straw" targets for rhetorical assault. In light of the geopolitical discussion of the previous chapters, what follows is an attempt, first, to identify the proper relationships among maritime and other kinds of strategies and, second, to outline alternative concepts for US national security policy that could guide the process of strategy selection.

At this juncture it is essential to comment briefly on the purpose of seapower. Admiral Wylie states that "the maritime theory":

> . . . consists, briefly, of two major parts: the establishment of control of the sea, and the exploitation of the control of the sea toward establishment of control on the land.[1]

Much of the contemporary debate about the US Navy's Maritime Strategy pertains not to the matter of control of the sea lines of communication—the plain necessity for that is unversally recognized, though there is quite impassioned debate over exactly how much control can best be ensured—but rather to the offensive value against Soviet landpower of Western preponderance at sea. If the armies of the maritime alliance of the West, perhaps with the invaluable distractive assistance of a Chinese co-belligerent, cannot conceive seriously of following in the footsteps of Napoleon and Hitler on the road to Moscow, how—and where—would a prolonged seige of the Soviet continental imperium be prosecuted? Answers are not hard to provide, but maritime strategies, and the US Navy's Maritime Strategy, require explicit development in the realm of Wylies's second major part—the exploitation of sea control on the land.

It is noticeable that many of the proponents of the Maritime Strategy tend to wax impatient with questions that probe "how" and "where" seapower would or might be employed flexibly, with surprise, so as to concentrate force by maneuver on a global scale against the vulnerable flanks of the Soviet fortress. It is no less noticeable that critics of the Maritime Strategy have a way of asserting that, while seapower can be a nuisance (e.g., it can raid), it cannot reach far enough inland with a sufficiency in strength for decisive effect. To date there has been too much theory and too

---

[1] Wylie, *Military Strategy*, p. 39.

little careful historical study or future-oriented middle and end-game analysis of the "trailing edge" of prolonged conflict, on all sides of the seapower-landpower debate.

MARITIME AND NATIONAL MILITARY STRATEGY

This is a discussion of strategy in relation to the military missions that the geopolitical context of US national security suggests should be important over the long haul. The practical viability of a strategy, however, has to be established with respect to its political acceptability and its tactical feasibility. Effectiveness in a national security undertaking is the product of an application of a sufficient quantity and quality of military power, with suitable military method, in pursuit of achieveable goals that would contribute to the ends of high policy. Effectiveness will be elusive, and may be impossible, if there are serious weaknesses in any of the links in the chain just described. In other words, US national security policy may not succeed if:

1. It requires the armed forces to accomplish the exceedingly difficult or impossible. This was probably true for Germany in both World Wars, was certainly true for Japan in 1941–45, and may have been true for the United States in Vietnam.[2]
2. Strategies, or plans of action, are selected which, even if successful, do not advance achievement of the political goals set by policy.
3. The quantity and quality of military power developed is insufficient to implement strategy.[3]

---

[2] One of the most interesting questions about Vietnam is whether the US Army could have won, given the political facts that the Johnson Administration was not seeking the military overthrow of North Vietnam and, therefore, was not prepared to sanction ground forces' action on a large scale beyond the boundaries of South Vietnam. I am sympathetic to the proposition that the US Army, with different strategic direction and better tactics, probably could have achieved some functional equivalent of victory on domestically politically tolerable terms. For a contrasting view, see Edward N. Luttwak, *The Pentagon and the Art of War* (New York: Simon and Schuster, 1984), Chapters 1–2. Luttwak argues that the US armed forces were — and remain — incapable of waging war successfully. A work of outstanding value is General Bruce Palmer, Jr., *The 25–Year War: America's Military Role in Vietnam* (Lexington, KY: University Press of Kentucky, 1984).

[3] See Martin van Creveld, *Fighting Power: German and US Army Performance, 1939–1945* (Westport, CT: Greenwood Press, 1982).

4. A war is insufficiently popular.[4]

Recognition of interdependencies among the above levels of analysis, and nuanced appreciation of the limits to rational defense planning, are not prominent features on the landscape of the contemporary US domestic defense debate. Too much of the public heat of debate is focused upon disconnected elements which, though important in and of themselves as contributors to, and constituents of, properly framed arguments, nonetheless serve to detract from the overall quality of debate. Opinions differ over the extent of allied enthusiasm for the common defense; while in addition, there is an on-going debate over the identity of, and meaning of the distinctions among, *survival, vital,* and *major* US national interests.

In the absence of a sound understanding of the geopolitical structure of US security, many people do not recognize why Rimland Eurasia, as a barrier against the Soviet Union, protects North America through its ability to deny Moscow the means and the opportunity to use preponderant landpower as the basis for a bid for preponderant seapower (and air-seapower). Even if that point is comprehended, there is widespread conviction that strategic nuclear weapons would render a Fortress America cost-effectively defensible. That proposition, which could become quite popular in the years immediately ahead, will require very careful geopolitical refutation.

In a stimulating essay in defense of US interventionism, Charles Krauthammer conceded the strategic logic of the neo-isolationist argument: "In fact, alliances are a threat to US security. They make the United States risk its own national existence for interests (like Europe) on which its physical security does not depend."[5] Krauthammer finds himself obliged to take refuge in ideology:

---

[4] The point is emphasized in Harry G. Summers, Jr., *On Strategy: A Critical Analysis of the Vietnam War* (Novato, CA: Presidio Press, 1982); Palmer, *The 25-Year War;* and by Caspar W. Weinberger as the fifth of his "six major tests to be applied when the United States is considering committing US forces to combat." *Annual Report to the Congress, Fiscal Year 1987* (Washington, DC: US Government Printing Office, February 5, 1986), p. 78. The Secretary of Defense advises that: "Before the United States commits combat forces abroad, the US Government should have some reasonable assurance of the support of the American people and their elected representatives." (p. 79). Weinberger has been greatly criticized for specifying impractical prerequisites. This author believes that Weinberger's position is by far the superior one. If US strategy and political culture are out of step, policy will fail.
[5] Charles Krauthammer, "Isolationism, Left And Right," *The New Republic,* March 4, 1985, p. 25.

The ultimate response, therefore, to right isolationism must be the assertion that an alliance of free nations, as the locus and trustee of Western values, is a value in itself. In other words, the answer to right isolationism must be Wilsonian.[6]

It is a thesis of this monograph that, while Krauthammer's argument for the necessity or strong desirability of a superpower United States assuming a global guardian role for Western civilization—*qua* values—is important and probably valid, there is no need for it to be compelled to bear the weight of traffic in argument that he suggests. To repeat a theme advanced here, there would be no true security in a Fortress America. A US withdrawal, more or less selectively, from the multilateral and bilateral security structures erected for containment purposes in the late 1940s and 1950s would alter the global correlation of forces in the Soviet favor. The United States would risk a precipitate ''bandwagon'' effect, as attentive former security clients and neutrals saw the direction in which history was tending,[7] and the geopolitical terms of the superpower contest would be altered greatly to the US disadvantage. Indeed, it would be difficult to imagine any US policy shift more likely to encourage hegemonism in Soviet statecraft than such a US retreat in fear. It should not be forgotten that a decision to defend America much closer to home than previously could hardly help but be perceived abroad exactly for what it would be: an expression of fear and a loss of nerve and courage on the part of the United States.

Commentators on strategy may need reminding that oceans and oceanic distances do not have inherent, permanent strategic meaning. Stated directly, oceans may divide or they may connect, depending upon the balance of advantage in relative maritime power. Absolute distance always must be a factor in the application or projection of power, but in and of itself it affords no protection. Armed forces necessarily have more combat power the closer they are to their bases, but—as the US Navy demonstrated on a transoceanic scale in the Pacific War, 1941–45—maritime power can build new, advanced bases and can maintain at sea floating bases

---

[6] *Ibid.*

[7] The ''bandwagon'' effect is challenged, implausibly, in Walt, ''Alliance Formation and the Balance of World Power.''

adequate for most combat support functions. As with the Channel in British history, the value of the Atlantic and Pacific oceans as defensive moats for the United States in the future depends entirely upon the relative maritime strengths of the superpowers. Spanish, French, and German designs and attempts to invade Britain failed uniformly for centuries, not because Britain is an island, but because, in the words of Sir Julian Corbett, "invasion over an uncommanded sea" was not a practical operation of war.[8] In World War II the Imperial Japanese Navy foolishly sought to enhance national security by providing a perimeter defense very far removed from the home islands. The Japanese forgot that a perimeter barrier of weakly held and mutually ill-supporting island "fortresses" could only be as strong as the mobile reserve (i.e., the navy) available and able to concentrate in a timely fashion for its protection.[9]

Although it is a necessary truth that policy is the master of strategy, it is no less true to claim that foreign policy decisions must be based upon prudent and realistic calculation of the strategic problems that they may create or exacerbate. A US defense community that typically does not think in strategic terms or debate genuinely strategic questions is unlikely to be well equipped to advise the President and the Congress on the costs and benefits of shifts in foreign policy direction. It is appropriate that there should be debates over numbers of ships, aircraft, and missiles, over the merits of this

---

[8] Julian S. Corbett, *Some Principles of Maritime Strategy* (Annapolis, MD: Naval Institute Press, 1972; first pub. 1911), p. 259. Corbett hammers home the point as follows: "With our impregnable flotilla hold covered by an automatic concentration of battle squadrons off Ushant, his [Napoleon's] army could never even have put forth, unless he had inflicted upon our covering fleet such a defeat as would have given him command of the sea, and with absolute command of the sea the passage of an army presents no difficulties." (pp. 259–60). It was no accident—as Soviet writers are fond of saying—that France failed repeatedly in its endeavors to invade England. See Rene Daveluy, *The Genius of Naval Warfare, I: Strategy* (Annapolis, MD: US Naval Institute, 1910; first pub. 1901), pp. 142–90. Commander Daveluy (of the French Navy) explains why the invasion attempts of 1692, 1744, 1745, 1759, 1779 and mooted for 1797, all failed. Succinctly stated, the British Royal Navy had a time-tested method for thwarting invasion designs, and the centerpiece of that method was the concentration of force with the weather gauge off Ushant. See Alfred T. Mahan, *The Influence of Sea Power Upon the French Revolution and Empire, 1793–1812, Vol. 1* (Boston: Little, Brown, 1898; first pub. 1892), pp. 338–46, and *Vol. 2*, pp. 118–21. Also see the maps illustrating the Ushant position in Julian S. Corbett, *The Campaign of Trafalgar* (London: Longman, Green, 1910), pp. 184, 302.

[9] This criticism pervades Paul S. Dull, *A Battle History of The Imperial Japanese Navy (1941–1945)* (Annapolis, MD: Naval Institute Press. 1978).

or that program as a "bargaining chip" for the arms control process, or over alleged "waste, fraud, and mismanagement" by the Department of Defense. True strategy argument, however, is noticeable for its rarity.[10] Military means make sense only in terms of policy ends, and the bridge between two, requiring two-way traffic, is strategy.[11]

Basic national security policy carries strong implications for, but by no means predetermines, choices in national military strategy. Study of American political culture, and its derivative "strategic culture," married to broad judgments about trends in political attitudes and behavior, suggests strongly that the United States in practice will have two classes of options for its basic national security policy through the remainder of this century: variants of containment and variants of withdrawal. Two additional classes of options should be cited for the sake of typological comprehensiveness: variants of "rollback" and variants of condominium—but these are believed by the author to be wholly impractical politically.[12]

Containment is by definition a defensive policy, at least in the near term, but its several purposes may be advanced by offensive political tactics, just as the strategic defensive does not preclude the tactical offensive. The overriding proximate purposes of containment is to hold what we (the US-organized and supported elements of the contemporary international order) have, and certainly to deny Western or neutral geopolitical assets to the Soviet imperium. However, it is recognized in the West both that effective, negative (if not passive) containment buys time for the evolution of the Soviet system, while a more active process of containment may provide fuel for benign change in the Soviet system.[13] More realistically perhaps, an active containment policy may seek to provide important distractions for Soviet energy, thereby reducing the energy available for application against the Western Alliance (obvious examples

---

[10] This is one of the less controversial claims advanced in Luttwak, *The Pentagon and the Art of War.*

[11] "The essential notion of strategy is captured in the relationship of means to ends — the combination of purpose and policies that guide the enterprise." Weinberger, *Annual Report to the Congress, Fiscal Year 1987,* p. 33.

[12] These national security policy concepts are treated in detail in Gray, *Geopolitics, Strategic Culture, and National Security,* Chapters 9–12.

[13] See Richard Pipes, *Survival Is Not Enough: Soviet Realities and America's Future* (New York: Simon and Schuster, 1984).

would include security-tie dalliance with Beijing, military assistance for Afghan, Angolan, Nicaraguan, *et al.,* freedom-fighters, and the encouragement of political destabilization in Poland.)

On October 24, 1985, President Reagan enunciated before the United Nations General Assembly what has come to be known, inevitably, as "the Reagan Doctrine." The President declared, in effect, that it was open season on the Soviet extended empire in South Asia, Southeast Asia, Africa, and Central America. Having stated a willingness to negotiate, or help negotiate, solutions to problems of regional conflict, the President proceeded to affirm that:

> Of course, until such times as these negotiations result in definitive progress, America's support for struggling democratic resistance forces must not and shall not cease.[14]

Notwithstanding the President's sincerity, his Doctrine has met with considerable resistance within the ranks of the government bureaucracy, as well as from a Congress both haunted by memories of Vietnam and professedly distressed that some of Mr. Reagan's free world insurgents do not resemble Jeffersonian democrats. Overall, application of pressure against the Soviet Union in the developing world must usefully increase the already very noticeable Soviet costs of empire.[15] Furthermore, Soviet imperial outposts in South and Southeast Asia, the Horn of Africa and Southern Africa, and in the Caribbean and Central America, are potentially of great distractive value for a Soviet Union that would seek, in time of war, to hinder the free use of the seas by the maritime alliance of the West.

Some Soviet clients in the third world undoubtedly would endeavor to remain neutral in an East-West conflict; whether or not they would be able to do so has to be matter for speculation. Of course Soviet and Soviet-client state forces operating in the third world would comprise only an irritant to West in the full context of a protracted war. Given the critical timing associated with the planned US reinforcement flow to NATO-Europe, however, a Soviet submarine campaign in the Florida Straits area, for example, albeit

---

[14] "The President's Message of Hope at the General Assembly of the United Nations," *Congressional Record,* Extension of Remarks, October 24, 1985, p. E4790.

[15] See Charles Wolf, Jr. et al., *The Costs of the Soviet Empire,* R-3073/1–NA (Santa Monica, CA: RAND, September 1983).

very minor in absolute terms and rapidly concluded by the US Navy, *could* make the difference between success and failure on the ground in Europe.

The 600-ship Navy currently under construction is a minimum for the global, forward, coalition-supportive strategy of the United States. For the Soviet Union, the geostrategic value of eminently expendable clients in the Caribbean and Central America is glaringly obvious. Those clients flank the US sea lines of communications to Europe, to the Middle East and to Asia both via the Atlantic route —round the Cape of Good Hope—and through the Panama Canal.

MULTILATERAL CONTAINMENT

In principle, a guiding policy concept of containment is consistent with three classes of preference concerning explicit foreign security commitments: multilateral, bilateral, and unilateral. The mutilateral, collective, or coalition approach to containment has been pursued by the United States since 1949 with NATO, for a while with SEATO, somewhat off-stage from formal membership with the long defunct Baghdad Pact-CENTO, and still with ANZUS (notwithstanding contemporary difficulties with New Zealand). The potential benefits of collective security are virtually self-evident. The United States has, in its column, countries more or less critically situated geographically to deny the Soviet Union access to the North Atlantic and the Pacific. Moreover, in addition to providing strategic territory for forward defense, the NATO-European countries contribute in absolute terms large quantities to Western ready military power.[16]

The price of collective security, however, is by no means cheap. Alliance-wide decisions have to reflect compromise among policies preferred by each member from its own parochial, if perhaps locally valid, perspective. The military arrangements for the defense of NATO-Europe flow not so much from a rational analysis of how

---

[16] For details see *The Military Balance, 1985–1986*, pp. 186–87. A most valuable recent study is Laurence Martin, *NATO and the Defense of the West: An Analysis of America's First Line of Defense* (New York: Holt, Rinehart and Winston, 1985). Martin notes that: "In the European theatre and surrounding oceans European members of NATO provide 90% of the ground forces, 90% of the armored divisions, 80% of the tanks, 80% of combat aircraft and 70% of combat naval vessels. Europe's military manpower numbers some 3 million active forces and 3 million reservists; the corresponding figure for the United States is 2 million active and 1 million reserve." (p. 121).

best the alliance could thwart Soviet designs in war, but rather more from the bequests of the thirty-six years of coalition history. These arrangements have not been updated to adjust suitably to a cumulatively dramatic, unfavorable shift in the multi-level military balance between East and West. Understandably enough, NATO-Europe:

1. Sees security more in terms of a visible strength and steadiness of US commitment than in persuasive architecture and detail for actual military defense.
2. Does not, indeed cannot, have a concept of "theater war" in Europe. NATO-Europe knows or believes that it would be the immediate battlefield. US concerns for a global strategy, and interest in preserving a sanctuary status for North America, generally are viewed in Europe with little enthusiasm (to be polite). US-authored strategic theory intended to develop a more powerful war-fighting design *for deterrence,* tends to be discounted in Europe as being founded upon a desire to limit the US liability (contrary to the spirit and even the letter of the 1949 NATO Treaty), and to be discouraged on the grounds that risk-bounding for the United States also means risk-bounding for the Soviet Union.
3. Is concerned that US containment policy outside of Europe might function, Sarajevo-like, to detonate a catastrophe in the NATO area.
4. Seeks both security against the Soviet threat and political/psychological reassurance against the prospect of war.[17] In practice, these needs can be, to an important degree, mutually exclusive.

Endeavors to identify, negotiate, and implement strategically rational defense plans for the Western Alliance suffer from recurring and debilitating sources of essentially political interdiction. First, the European members of the coalition, without exception, see in the magic formula of "flexible response" a framework for *pre-war deterrence* that works through the manipulation of Soviet perceptions of risk. The more plausible the prospect of a conflict in Europe escalating rapidly so as to engage the homelands of the superpowers

---

[17] See Michael Howard, "Reassurance and Deterrence: Western Defense in the 1980s," *Foreign Affairs,* vol. 61, no. 1 (Winter 1982–83), pp. 309–24.

and their so-called central strategic systems, the more robust is the deterrence barrier to war, or so the European aspiration insists. There are important local reasons why NATO-Europe repeatedly has declined to dedicate a suitable, affordable fraction of its ample resources to providing a local military capability so formidable that the burden of decision to escalate should be placed on Soviet shoulders.[18]

Second, supporting the first point, is the body of strategic theory which suggests that nuclear weapons have overthrown utterly the meaning and character of warfare, as warfare has been understood for the entire duration of recorded history. With respect to possible major military conflict between East and West, so the story proceeds, one can, or should, no longer think of force within the traditional framework of military theory. Armed forces will be deployed and, *in extremis,* used not in search of victory, or even to deny victory to the enemy, but rather to signal resolve and to provide some objective basis to enemy fears that Armageddon is nigh. The well-written contemporary tracts on nuclear strategy by Lawrence Freedman in Britain and Robert Jervis in the United States[19]—building on the foundations laid in the later 1950s and the 1960s by Thomas Schelling and Bernard Brodie[20]—in effect deny the military utility of nuclear force (and thereby do very great violence to the logic in the arguments of Clausewitz).[21]

---

[18] The Western difficulty may well be more political than economic. Helmut Schmidt, former Chancellor of the Federal Republic of Germany, believes that: ''If France would bring its conventional forces and reserves into the joint framework of Western defense, it would be easy to achieve a satisfactory equilibrium in conventional forces between Western Europe and the Soviet Union.'' *A Grand Strategy for the West: The Anachronism of National Strategies in an Interdependent World* (New Haven, CT: Yale University Press, 1985) p. 42. See David S. Yost, *France and Conventional Defense in Central Europe* (Boulder, CO: Westview Press, 1985).

[19] Respectively, Freedman, *The Evolution of Nuclear Strategy,* and Jervis, *The Illogic of American Nuclear Strategy.*

[20] Thomas C. Schelling, *The Strategy of Conflict* (Cambridge, MA: Harvard University Press, 1960); *Arms and Influence* (New Haven, CT: Yale University Press, 1966). Bernard Brodie, ed., *The Absolute Weapon: Atomic Power and World Order* (New York: Harcourt, Brace, 1947); *Strategy in the Missile Age* (Princeton, NJ: Princeton University Press, 1959); *Escalation and the Nuclear Option* (Princeton, NJ: Princeton University Press, 1966); *War and Politics* (New York: Macmillan, 1973).

[21] But, see—in its admittedly atrocious English language version—Raymond Aron, *Clausewitz: Philosopher of War* (London: Routledge and Kegan Paul, 1984), Part V. Aron claims that: ''As the almost legendary ancestor of Moltke and Schlieffen, Clausewitz belongs (provisonally) to a bygone age, at least if we are talking about relations between the great

In sum, a United States seeking to contain the Soviet hegemonic drive has to contend with geostrategically key allies who have theoretical cover for insisting, in practice, upon defense preparations that draw a highly dubious distinction between deterrence and defense.

BILATERAL CONTAINMENT

Without explicitly foreswearing multilateral military diplomacy, the United States could choose, for the long term, to reinforce, or forge new, bilateral security connections with countries of particular strategic value. Leading contenders for special US attention must be Britain, West Germany, Norway, and Turkey in Europe, and China and Japan in Northeast Asia.[22] It should be noted that there is a special quality already to US bilateral security relations with Britain, Germany, Norway, and Turkey, while US security relations with China, such as they are, and with Japan, are fairly strictly bilateral in character already. The high geostrategic value of these countries to the United States necessarily renders them of extraordinary geostrategic importance as targets for neutralization by the Soviet Union.

The public rhetoric of wartime diplomacy that emanated from Washington in the period 1941–45 was replete with references to free world allies, the newly conceived United Nations, and collective security. Yet the reality was that the United States took serious notice of the views of only one other country in Europe, Great Britain; while in its conduct of war in the Pacific the United States took serious notice of no country's views other than its own. After the fall of Malaya and Singapore, the British Royal Navy lacked the capacity to act in the Far East (having been withdrawn, of absolute necessity, to Ceylon—and even to East Africa—and Australia), while Washington never even pretended to treat the Austra-

---

powers.'' (p. 404). According to Lawrence Freedman, ''By the mid-1980s, therefore, four decades after the destruction of Hiroshima and Nagasaki, the nuclear strategists had still failed to come up with any convincing methods of employing nuclear weapons should deterrence fail that did not wholly offend common sense, nor had they even reached a consensus on whether or not the discovery of such methods was essential if deterrence was to endure.'' ''The First Two Generations of Nuclear Strategists,'' in Paret, ed., *Makers of Modern Strategy*, p. 778.

[22] The case for a special defense relationship with Canada is so obvious as to require no discussion here.

lian and New Zealand governments as equal allies. (In the Combined Chiefs of Staff forum in Washington, and at a series of Anglo-American heads-of-government conferences, Britain at least had some very limited ability to influence the course of the Pacific War. British influence was, however, essentially and insistently negative, attempting to minimize the US effort in the Pacific, pending decision against Germany in Europe.) The most important element of bilateralism in the American conduct of the Pacific War was not between countries, but rather was between the US Navy and the US Army.

Should the multilateral security arrangements of recent decades come unraveled — for whatever combination of reasons — a policy of global and geostrategically forward containment might still be feasible. It is asserted from time to time that, in US strategic perspective, NATO is really a US-German alliance. There is some sense in this assertion. West Germany is extraordinarily exposed to danger; as a consequence, it is extraordinarily dependent upon the security provided for it by the strongest member of NATO, the United States. Moreover, the US strategic position in peninsular Europe would not be viable, in any dimension, without a friendly government in Bonn. Nonetheless, for reasons of strategic geography, history, and culture, the key country for US security in the ''European theater'' is Great Britain.

It is probably no exaggeration to say that if Britain were to leave NATO, for example because a Labor Government deemed the nuclear policies of the alliance to be intolerable,[23] there would be a terminal weakening in the Atlanticist consensus that sustains the NATO commitment within the US political system. The US military commitment to NATO-Europe always has been contingent upon NATO-Europe behaving in a manner perceived by Americans as reflective of a strong desire to resist the common foe to the East. No American President would be likely to succeed in explaining to the American people and Congress that a trans-Atlantic arrangement for collective security was worthy of continuing American adherence without British participation. In terms of strategic geography, a

---

[23] The leader of Britain's Labor Party, Neil Kinnock, is not far removed in his opinions from the current stance of the Government of New Zealand. The Labor Party would seem to favor NATO as a conventional-forces alliance, at least as far as Britain is concerned. US ''nuclear bases'' in Britain would be an issue on which a Kinnock-led government would be expected by his back-benchers to take early action.

NATO already deprived of the certain availability of French territory, ports, and airspace, would be a plain military absurdity if
Britain's attitude were one of strict neutrality or worse. The Western
maritime approaches to Central and Northern Europe are commanded by British strategic geography, as statesmen as diverse as
Philip II of Spain, Louis XIV, Napoleon, and Hitler all could attest.

This discussion of a possible bilateral orientation in US containment policy should not encourage the view that the United States
would be very much at liberty, in nearly all cases, to pick and
choose the allies of greatest value and convenience. Great Britain,
one may be sure, would prefer a US security guarantee to no such
guarantee, irrespective of the character of a broader US security
policy for Europe as a region. British statesmen know just how
narrow the Channel and even the North Sea have become in the
twentieth century. One may be sure that British governments would
do all in their power to persuade the United States not to define a
new containment or blockade perimeter for Soviet power in Europe
strictly as having an offshore character.

On the other side of the world, the United States must be very
strongly interested in exploiting Japanese geography strategically
for the blockade of Soviet maritime assets in the North Pacific. Such
a blockade would protect China's oceanic flank and should help
encourage China to behave in ways that would discourage the Soviet
Union from swinging military forces from Central Asia and Siberia
for employment in Europe (as Stalin was able to do for the defense
of Moscow and the launching of his first great Winter offensive in
December 1941.) Bilateral though the several US security arrangements may be in Northeast Asia, the United States would discover
that were it to attempt to divest itself of its long-extant commitment
to the territorial integrity of South Korea, the reaction in Tokyo and
in Beijing would be very negative. American strategic planners and
commentators should remember that the Japanese are as sensitive
to adverse security developments in the Korean peninsula, as the
British have been *vis à vis* the Low Countries (Flanders and Antwerp
in particular). One might recall that the proximate *casus belli* for
the Russo-Japanese War of 1904–05 was a Russian move to secure
hegemony over Korea. Furthermore, from the geostrategic perspective of Beijing, a strong US military posture in Japanese and
South Korean territory and waters, preferably with considerable

offensive potential, is a vitally important constraint upon Soviet freedom of action against the Chinese heavy industrial base in Manchuria.

These examples, focusing upon the geostrategic offshore "twins" of Britain and Japan, are intended simply to illustrate the historically enduring general truth that when one enlists allies, even very selectively and on a nominally bilateral basis, one also incurs at least some obligation to be sensitive to their unique geopolitical perspectives.

There is always the danger that readers will deduce more from a silence in analysis than is intended. By any standards of size and location of strategic geography, as well as scale and quality of political, economic, and military assets, there can be no question but that France is a very important member of the Western Alliance — notwithstanding its post-1966 absence from the military organization of NATO. However, it is the judgment of the author that France, relatively speaking, is not as important as Britain or West Germany as a bilateral security partner for the United States. Without Britain or West Germany, NATO, if it could survive at all — which would be very problematical — would be a very different alliance. No similar claim can be advanced concerning France.

In 1985, for the first time, the French Government formally adopted a policy of extended nuclear deterrence for West German territory. Furthermore, it is a fairly open secret that French policymakers genuinely are concerned that West German leaders should see in the Franco-German alliance a robust alternative both to a US-dominated NATO nexus that may one day prove politically fragile, and to some variant of entente with the East (shades of Rapallo, 1922).[24] It would be easy for a cynical American policymaker to see in French diplomacy little more than a bid for greater regional influence. However, there are grounds for believing that France truly is anxious over the long-term direction that might be adopted by West German policy and is seeking to help preclude any German return to "rogue elephant" behavior. It can be argued that the now long-standing French security stance of independence functions to the net benefit of the Western Alliance. Nonetheless, the facts re-

---

[24] See Roland Smith, *Soviet Policy Towards Germany,* Adelphi Papers no. 203 (London: IISS, Winter 1985).

main that France has starved its conventional forces of resources for many years in pursuit of a technically viable independent deterrent (the *force de frappe*), and that the uncertainties deliberately promoted by French security policy could work either to strengthen or to detract from deterrence in Europe.[25] On balance, this author inclines to believe the latter.

UNILATERAL CONTAINMENT

Having discussed multilateral and bilateral approaches to the US containment of Soviet power, a brief review of the unilateralist alternative is in order.[26] This is one of those many subjects in security debates that lends itself so easily to ridicule and peremptory dismissal that it is rarely considered fairly. It would seem reasonable to observe that a unilateralist approach in US security policy most probably is incompatible with a guiding policy concept of containment—or, at least, of containment on-shore in Eurasia. This is not quite true.

Unilateralism, empathetically if not sympathetically appraised, implies not so much a US determination to act alone, unilaterally, as rather a determination not to permit some friends and allies to deny the United States the ability to act as, when, and where US policy calculation deems essential in defense of vital US interests.[27] There is, of course, a potential central tension between the unilateralist option and alliance ties. Given the partial-family character of NATO, risks run by the United States in the conduct of a unilateral venture would be risks in some measure shared by US allies. This discussion must register the point explicitly that leadership of the Western Alliance is of net security benefit to the United States. It

---

[25] See David S. Yost, *France's Deterrent Posture and Security in Europe: Part I: Capabilities and Doctrines,* and *Part II: Strategic and Arms Control Implications,* Adelphi Papers nos. 194–195 (London: IISS, Winter 1984/85). A provocative treatment of French defense policy by the most gifted of France's younger strategic thinkers is Pierre Lellouche, *L'Avenir de la guerre* (Paris: Editions Mazanine, 1985).

[26] See Keith A. Dunn and William O. Staudenmaier, *Strategic Implications of the Continental-Maritime Debate,* The Washington Papers no. 107 (New York: Praeger [with the Georgetown Center for Strategic and International Studies], 1984), pp. 14–16. For a moderate unilateralist tract, see Jeffrey Record, *Revising US Military Strategy: Tailoring Means to Ends* (Washington, DC: Pergamon-Brassey's, 1984).

[27] For a very blunt development of this point, see Charles Krauthammer, "The Multilateralist Fallacy," *The New Republic,* December 9, 1985, pp. 17–20.

is recognized here also, though, that the geostrategic benefit of the alliance structure does not come as a "free good" to the United States.

Sensibly framed, the unilateralist perspective should be stated as a determination to secure for the United States such freedom of unilateral policy action as it may occasionally need, to the extent possible consistent with the integrity of the terms and conditions of alliance maintenance. The basis of unilateralist reasoning is the following:

1. The United States, alone among Western countries, is a truly global power.

2. In the global competition for relative advantage of position, which is one way of characterizing Soviet-American antagonism in geopolitical terms, only the United States among the Western (and Asian) allies has the capacity to act "out of area" on more than a very modest scale.[28]

3. Although all the NATO allies pay lip-service to the strategic significance of "out of area" issues, in practice, their eyes, like their strategic assets, are locked firmly onto local dangers. NATO-Europe would like to decouple regional instabilities in the Middle East, Asia, Central America, and so forth, from the politics of security in Europe. As a NATO member possibly acting vigorously "out of area," the United States, with the global unity of her behavior, couples security in Europe to dangers in distant places. It follows that, in practice, the NATO-European allies can function as a serious drag upon an American policy that uniquely is obliged to take a global view of security threats.

4. The politics of security assurance and reassurance in NATO have obliged the United States to purchase and sustain a very heavily Europe-oriented military force posture. This may be criticized on three complementary grounds. First, an unhealthily large fraction of (supposedly) general purpose military power is tied down in, or is committed to, the forward, on-shore defense of NATO-Europe, and hence is (admittedly variably — as the Vietnam War demon-

---

[28] A constructive recent discussion of this subject is William T. Tow, "NATO's Out-Of-Region Challenges and Extended Containment," *Orbis*, vol. 28, no. 4 (Winter 1985), pp. 829–55. Also see Gregory F. Treverton, *Making the Alliance Work: The United States and Western Europe* (Ithaca, NY: Cornell University Press, 1985), Chapter 4.

strated) unavailable for use elsewhere in the world. Second, the balance among and within the armed services reflects the prospective fighting priorities for a large war in Central Europe. Third, the character and missions of the US armed forces do not reflect, strictly, what must follow from the NATO commitment. There is no inexorable military necessity for the US Army to deploy heavy armored divisions in defense of the inner-German border, or to stockpile so much matériel (six POMCUS sets) for marriage with American reinforcing (Reforger) divisions. These arrangements are substantially political in purpose. The NATO "layer cake" national corps defense design was, and remains, intended to deny the reality, or even the appearance of the possibility, of the Soviet Union moving westwards against West Germany alone. Furthermore, military deployments do have political significance in perceptions. A degree of US disengagement from forward ground defense in Central Europe, no matter how sensibly intended to effect a strategically rational reallocation of defense tasks within the Alliance, inevitably would be interpreted as a lessening of US political commitment to NATO-Europe.[29]

Unilateralism can be advanced as an expression of frustration with the inability of the United States to act as effectively as it feels it must out of the NATO area, because of the political and military constraints imposed by the alliance as it functions, and as it is organized militarily. Alternatively (and far preferably), unilateralism can be advanced as a desirable adjustment to a changing geostrategic context. Without denying the political logic, for deterrence in Soviet minds and for the reassurance of allies, of very visible toward military deployment in Central Europe, the United States could argue that the objective material conditions for a more equal security partnership between America and Europe now exist. The point could be made that it is very wasteful of scarce resources for

---

[29] Secretary of Defense Weinberger states that: "In Europe, for example, our mobility programs are building toward a capability to deploy six combat divisions and 60 tactical fighter squadrons by ten days after mobilization, thereby enhancing NATO's posture." *Annual Report to the Congress, Fiscal Year 1987*, p. 52. One need not be a unilateralist, let alone an isolationist, to see some merit in the following point made by Eliot Cohen: "Military logic suggests the peculiarity (at the very least) of a strategy which relies heavily on the appearance within a week of massive armies from a power thousands of miles distant from the main battle front." "Do We Still Need Europe?", p. 35.

the United States to continue to assume a heavy ground defense role in Europe on the contemporary scale, given the material and financial ability of NATO-Europe to provide most of the necessary local fighting power at much less cost.

A unilateralist perspective is one that anticipates the possibility of the United States acting substantially alone. It need not imply US action over the opposition of NATO allies; it need not preclude allied approval; and it need not require restructuring and redeployment of the US armed forces. However, this orientation in containment policy does imply a US willingness to act without alliance-wide approval, even in the face of considerable opposition. Moreover, to the degree to which it may lead to a more active US policy out of the NATO area, the US armed forces could not be permitted to be so specialized in capability, or so restricted politically in their deployment options, that additional commitments beyond Europe would be extraordinarily difficult.

WITHDRAWAL

By way of sharp contrast in purpose with a policy of containment —in its many variants of multilateralism, bilateralism, and unilateralism—a policy of withdrawal would be intended, to the extent geostrategically feasible, to remove the United States from harm's way. Withdrawal, neo-isolationism, Fortress America—whatever the preferred description—would change dramatically the geopolitical referents for rival positions in the US defense debate, but not the fact of such a debate. From the point of view of US defense policy and the framers of national military strategy, where would lie the outer defensive works of Fortress America? Presumably a policy rationale for withdrawal to the Americas would have to mean the redrawing of a US defense perimeter around ''the Americas'' north of the equator—so Fortress America would include Canada in the north and Venezuela and Colombia in the south.

US security retirement to the Western Hemisphere need not imply a revival in application of the Monroe Doctrine. In the Spring of 1982 the US Government demonstrated by its actions where the balance of US interests lay between Britain and Argentina. South America below the equator is, and is likely long to remain, geostrategically very remote from the principal axes of US-Soviet en-

gagement. However, the prudent US defense planner should anticipate that the geostrategic meaning of South America likely would
change, albeit probably rather slowly, in the security context specified here. In short, if the United States were to dismantle her trans-
Atlantic security commitments, then — sooner or later — the Soviet
Union would come to exercise effective control over littoral peninsular Europe, and Soviet strategic "reach" would continue a process of extension into Africa that already is well begun. Readers
should recall the Nazi German threat to the United States that
American geopoliticians predicted in the very early 1940s.[30] A Germany victorious in Eurasia would thereby have acquired the basis
for construction of the means to conduct a true *Weltpolitik*. It is easy
to frighten the credulous with large red arrows on small maps, but
the US body politic should not need reminding, in the mid-1980s
looking out to the early years of the next century, that it does not
have a stable backyard south of the border.

---

[30] See Spykman, *America's Strategy in World Politics.*

4

CHOICE OF STRATEGY

THE STRATEGIC CONTEXT

The national military strategy adopted and pursued by the United States should be congruent with the policy goals that justify that strategy. In practice, policy can be so vague or so influenced by a desire to stimulate particular domestic and foreign perceptions of will, that, in effect, it yields no guidance of real utility to defense planners. If the global containment of Soviet power is the central guiding purpose for US national security policy, with the proximate goal of denying Moscow a substantially unchallenged hegemony over Eurasia, then the framework for US strategy is not difficult to identify — though room remains for important debate over means and methods.

This author endorses both ideological and geostrategic rationales for a forward containment policy. Given that domestic American support for a prudent containment policy is keyed to official presentation of national security objectives in terms of values and ideology, and that politicians are expert manipulators of the appropriate symbols of cultural politics, the discussion here focuses upon the geostrategic rationales for policy and military strategy.

The maritime alliance of the West, being strategically on the defensive, enjoys what is known as the ''defender's advantage'' in motivation: that is to say that Western countries should be more strongly committed to holding what they have than the Soviet Union should be to secure gains, *ceteris paribus*. The *caveat* is important. Advantages in relative capability, real or imagined, can more than compensate for a nominal asymmetry in political commitment (as the whole of recorded history reveals). Moreover, a general truth, such as the ''defender's advantage,'' is always vulnerable to falsification in particular cases. The leading generic scenarios for the outbreak of a major war between East and West come in four classes, and sidestep the ''defender's advantage'' in different ways:

1. *A Soviet crisis-of-empire.* The USSR strikes westwards in order to secure control of an external environment that is destabilizing its imperium.[1]
2. *War by miscalculaton.* War occurs after the manner of July-August 1914, as one event leads to another, with neither East nor West originally having intended to fight.
3. *War from a contemporary imbalance of power.* The ''defender's advantage'' is more than negated by a favorable ratio in military power on the side of the country on the strategic offensive (a ratio augmented by the force-multiplying effects of surprise). This favorable imbalance in military power leads the aggressor to believe that he can now control the risks he would be running.
4. *War in order to forestall a steep adverse decline in the balance of power (or correlation of forces).* The Soviet Union decides to fight now — as Japan did in 1941 — because the military-political balance is predicted with high confidence to decline very sharply against it in the years ahead. Provided military staffs have a persuasive story showing how victory is probable today, much of the usual inhibition against military adventure will be absent.[2]

---

[1] This is one, but only one, of the classic motives for imperial expansion. Empires as different in time and circumstance as the Roman and the British sought to protect their territorial empires by maintaining a measure of hegemonic control over paid/intimidated client states beyond the imperial frontiers. An outstanding relevant case study is Edward N. Luttwak, *The Grand Strategy of the Roman Empire: From the First Century A.D. to the Third* (Baltimore: Johns Hopkins University Press, 1976).

[2] If Thucydides is to be believed, this fourth scenario was the precipitating cause of the Peloponnesian War. ''The Spartans voted that the treaty had been broken and that war should be declared not so much because they were influenced by the speeches of their allies as because they were afraid of the further growth of Athenian power, seeing, as they did, that already the greater part of Hellas was under the control of Athens.'' *The Peloponnesian War* (London: Cassell, 1962), p. 62. The case of Japan cited in the text is one of the clearest examples in history of how a prudent rearmament program on the part of a *status quo* power, the United States, provided an exceedingly powerful incentive for a dissatisfied power to fight as soon as possible. The US Two-Ocean Naval Expansion Act of June 1940 — with

The geostrategic reality of the West's interrupted, on-shore containing line in Eurasia is considerably stronger than superficial study of a map could lead one to believe. In principle, the Soviet Union, utilizing the value of the initiative, could select vulnerable targets of opportunity that would not lend themselves easily to local defense. In practice, however, a flagrant act of Soviet aggression that was geostrategically very limited in its immediate goals would forfeit the potentially war-winning value of surprise in return for a modest gain. Successful local Soviet offensive action — against Norway or Turkey, for example — might trigger the unraveling of NATO, if NATO-Europe decided that the action in question demonstrated that the alliance could neither protect nor promise to liberate. Nonetheless, more probable results of Soviet aggression on so limited a scale would be general Western mobilization and, if time permitted, rearmament, and the conduct of a geographically unconstrained scale of military response at times and places of US or NATO choosing. In short, one important function of relatively weak forward defense is to compel the enemy to fight, albeit perhaps on a modest scale, and thereby declare the intensity of his intentions.

"Horizontal escalation" has not been debated competently in recent years. Execution of such escalation, it should be emphasized, would reflect the facts that attractive steps in vertical escalation would not be available and that the premier general-purpose force instrument of the maritime alliance, superior naval power, inherently is suitable for such missions (by way of contrast to heavy, mechanized Army formations). Critics of horizontal escalation point, correctly, both to the improbability of finding strategic compensation through gains on the Soviet flanks for the short-war loss of NATO territory in Central-Western Europe, and to the dangers of vertical escalation that would accompany horizontal escalation. But, overall, the critics have created a "straw target."[3] In the context of a stalemated NATO-Warsaw Pact ground war in Central Europe, hori-

---

construction to be completed in 1946–48—would preclude any prospect of naval victory for Japan in the Western Pacific. In the words of a British naval historian: "(T)he Two-Ocean Naval Expansion Act doomed the Imperial Navy to second-class status . . . . This was the argument that pushed Japan into war." H.P. Willmott, *Empires in The Balance: Japanese and Allied Pacific Strategies to April 1942,* (Annapolis, MD: Naval Institute Press, 1982), p. 61.

[3] For example, see Joshua M. Epstein, "Horizontal Escalation: Sour Notes of a Recurrent Theme," *International Security,* vol. 8, no. 3 (Winter 1983–84), pp. 19–31.

zontal escalation would be nothing more than common sense; while should NATO lose a ground war in Europe, a United States determined to continue the war would be compelled to pursue a peripheral strategy.

Far more troubling than any prospect of horizontal escalation on the part of the West, is the possibility of its exercise by a Soviet Union that chose to exploit the ''wrong footing'' of the United States in a region logistically far removed from Central Europe. Writing about US improvements in strategic mobility, Secretary of Defense Weinberger advises: ''Once these programs are complete, we will be able to deploy seven divisions in Southwest Asia.''[4] How would NATO-Europe be reinforced if US strategic air and sealift were fully employed sustaining a major expeditionary force in Southwest Asia? It may be sensible for the United States to be able to deploy a multi-division force to Southwest Asia—but not in the context of continuing NATO dependence upon US rapid reinforcement. One should recall the anxieties of 1950–51 as to whether or not Korea was ''the wrong war, at the wrong place, at the wrong time, and with the wrong enemy,'' in General Bradley's words (presumably this last point, at least, would not apply).[5]

The following points should not be neglected when one considers the national military strategy suitable for a United States determined to continue its long-standing policy of global containment.

First, the alternatives to a US national military strategy designed to deny as much as possible of Rimland Eurasia to Soviet hegemony, carry the risk of a Soviet Union in effective strategic command of littoral Eurasia and at substantial liberty, as a consequence, to initiate what would amount to a maritime siege of North America.

Second, surprise is not a reliable substitute for military muscle. It can be a force multiplier, but it is an eminently fragile quality in defense planning. NATO's theoretical vulnerability to surprise attack, should Pact forces wheel out of what appeared to be an exercise into an actual invasion, is well known. In practice, however, it is very unlikely that Soviet political and military leaders would either

---

[4] *Annual Report to the Congress, Fiscal Year 1987*, p. 52

[5] US Congress, Senate Committees on Armed Services and Foreign Relations, *Military Situation in the Far East, Hearings*, 82nd Cong., 1st sess. (Washington, DC: US Government Printing Office, 1951), pp. 731–32.

assume the achievement of strategic surprise or would rely upon its force multiplying efficacy to endure much beyond the first clash of arms.[6]

Third, in principle, though possibly not in practice, NATO has more than sufficient ready, and readily mobilizable (and transportable), military forces deployed on, and committed to, the Central Front so as to impose a relatively slow campaign of attrition on the Pact attacker.[7]

Fourth, Soviet forces might succeed in seizing northern Norway, but such an action would be far removed from securing reliable access to the North Atlantic. Soviet seizure of airfields and ports in the north of Norway would be a very great inconvenience to NATO and would place enormous strain on very limited British air defense assets, but would not necessarily preclude NATO's maintenance of an effective blockade in the Greenland-Iceland-United Kingdom (GIUK) gap. However, Soviet seizure of airfields south of Evenes (Narvik) would render a forward maritime strategy by NATO in the region increasingly hazardous.[8] In practice, the author believes that Soviet military power is more likely to be on the defensive than the offensive on the Northern Flank.[9]

Fifth, strategic geography in NATO's Southern Flank would seem to be designed to foster a stand-off. Pact forces might break through into the Mediterranean, but those that survived the first clash of arms, and those that might be surged forward once the barrier of NATO's Southern Flank had been ruptured, would be going nowhere of *near-term* strategic importance.

Sixth, Soviet forces in trans-Caucasia and Central Asia cer-

---

[6] As important as the imponderability of surprise would be the scale and efficacy of "surprise effect." See Basil H. Liddell Hart, *History of the First World War* (London: Pan Books, 1972; first pub. 1934), p. 325. This is a critical distinction that many scholars neglect.

[7] See Richard Ned Lebow, "The Soviet Offensive in Europe: The Schlieffen Plan Revisited?" *International Security*, vol. 9, no. 4 (Spring 1985), pp. 44–78

[8] A useful, admittedly high-morale, discussion is Hugh K. O'Donnell, Jr., "Northern Flank Maritime Offensive," *Proceedings*, vol. 111/9/991 (September 1985), pp. 42–57.

[9] But, NATO planners should not take undue comfort from the prospect of a favorable naval balance in the Norwegian Sea. It should be recalled that Germany, through boldness, deception, bluff, speed, and superiority in the air, seized strategic objectives in Norway in April 1940 despite the fact that the Royal Navy enjoyed an unchallengeable local command of the sea. Prospectively, the 1940 "analogy" should be invalidated by the ability of NATO to project maritime airpower ashore, even in the far north.

tainly could invade Iran and head for the Gulf and the Arabian Sea (though the terrain lends itself to defense), but, again, so what? It is most unlikely that the United States and her allies in Europe and Asia would accept any measure of *wartime* dependence upon Gulf oil that would require the forward defense of the Gulf oil-fields. If this is so, as it certainly should be, it has to follow that the US and allied navies need not plan to secure and maintain a quality of sea control suitable to protect tanker routes from the Gulf to Europe and Japan (preeminently). Soviet forces committed to the seizure and occupation of territory in the Middle East and Southwest Asia would be overextended forces committed to a theater of operations irrelevant to the outcome of a relatively short war and exposed to counterattack in the event of a protracted conflict.

The "two ocean" problem that Soviet strategic geography poses for the US Navy may be a dilemma for American uniformed planners and operators, but it is a net asset for the West of enormous significance. The Soviet Union has no choice other than to contemplate the prospect of a two(plus)-front war.[10] Even that definition is optimistic for Moscow, given that the Asian "front" encompasses, potentially, the entirety of the frontier with China and, more plausibly still, confrontation with an American military power anchored in South Korea and on an island chain reaching from Luzon in the Philippines, through Hokkaido in Japan, the Aleutians and then to Alaska—and expressed in the form of a manifestly superior (maritime) power projection capability. The importance in Soviet calculations of the second front in Asia (a certain second front with US maritime power and a possible second/third front *vis à vis* China) must depend upon how optimistically they would view the prospects for a rapid favorable decision in the West.

If Soviet leaders believe that their forces could inflict a definitive defeat upon NATO in Europe in the course of two-to-four weeks, and that Soviet nuclear capabilities would function reliably as a counterdeterrent, then even substantial military setbacks in the Far East, or along the Chinese frontier, could be endured temporarily. Indeed, in that context, Soviet anticipation of suffering considerable disadvantage in Asia should not serve very usefully to

---

[10] See General P.X. Kelley, "The Amphibious Warfare Strategy," in Watkins et al., *The Maritime Strategy,* p. 26.

enhance deterrence. But if Soviet leaders: were far from confident that a definitive theater victory in Europe would in practice be secured in days or a few weeks; feared that an undefeated (save in Europe) United States, undamaged at home, would choose and be able to continue to prosecute global war; or expected to suffer very great nuclear damage at home in the course of winning a campaign or war in Europe; then, the prospect of loss in the Far East would be of very considerable importance, and should enhance deterrence usefully.

Common sense, as well as contemporary defense reformers, reminds us that strategy is an exercise in the making of choices. In practice, many important choices are, and should be recognized as, foreordained by geopolitics. Moreover, as William Kaufmann insists, US freedom of action in choice of strategic objectives is somewhat constrained by the fact that the overall strategic posture, and certainly the political purpose of the Western Alliance, is defensive in character.[11] To the substantial degree to which the US/NATO choice of strategic objectives must flow from the scale, kind, locations, and assessed intentions of a Soviet attack, Western strategy is generically reactive in nature. The flexibility with which superior naval power can be applied is important in principle, as the United States and NATO seek to shape an overall strategy that leans on relative Western strengths and exploits relative Soviet weaknesses. But, the strategic value of superior naval power is *to a degree* offset by the very substantial inaccessibilty of the core areas of Soviet power to the direct application of pressure from the sea,[12] and the geostrategic vulnerability of peninsular Europe to the long-suit of Soviet power, mechanized ground forces.

The principal restriction upon choice of strategy for NATO and for the United States is geopolitical in nature. Whatever the US/NATO choice among military instruments and the operational methods chosen for their employment, the primary immediate objective of the alliance must be to defeat a Soviet invasion of West Germany.

---

[11] William W. Kaufmann, "Force Planning and Vietnam." Paper prepared for the USMA Senior Conference, "Vietnam-Did It Make A Difference?" West Point, New York, May 30–June 1, 1985, pp. 7, 13.

[12] Sir Halford Mackinder defined what first he termed "The Geographical Pivot of History," and later the "Heartland" of the "World Island" of Eurasia, in terms of its inaccessibility to seapower. See Mackinder, *Democratic Ideals and Reality,* pp. 241–64.

In so far as NATO is concerned, though not necessarily the United States as a separate national security community, Western Europe, from the Baltic to the Adriatic, does comprise prospectively the main theater of operations. Arguments over the implications of this inalienable fact dominate the recent debate over US national military strategy. Much of this debate — between self-described continentalists/coalitionists and maritime advocates[13]—has reflected considerable mutual misunderstanding (some, no doubt, willful in origin), the attacking of imaginary debating positions, and an absence of history-based prudence.[14] A US Navy-oriented analysis of the geostrategic situation of the West yields a number of propositions.

First, US (and allied) maritime advantage is not just desirable, but literally essential for the deterrence of war, in that the credible promise of the US exercise of sea control is a necessary precondition for the conduct of protracted armed conflict in and about Eurasia-Africa. Needless to add, perhaps, Western ability to enforce a long war on the Soviet Union could be defeated if US strategic nuclear forces were insufficient to impose escalation discipline, or if the United States was denied a sufficient quality of working control of the key sea lines of communication (SLOCs).

Second, if NATO's ground and tactical air forces go down in defeat in a matter of days, US and allied naval forces cannot provide immediate strategic compensation through the achievement of success of comparable strategic value elsewhere. Furthermore, NATO's

---

[13] The leading continentalist tract is Robert W. Komer, *Maritime Strategy or Coalition Defense?* (Cambridge, MA: Abt Books, 1984). There is no comparable extra-official work on the maritime side, though the closest approximation thereto probably is Record, *Revising US Military Strategy,* (notwithstanding Record's vigorously worded differences with some expressions of official Navy thinking.)

[14] Robert Komer, for example, has sought to clarify his opposition to current US maritime strategy by explaining: "My argument is that overinvestment in a carrier-heavy Navy at the expense of other capabilities could be tantamount to making it impossible to defend Europe, or the Persian Gulf, for that matter." "Comment and Discussion: 'Northern Flank Maritime Offensive'," *Proceedings,* vol. 112/1/995 (January 1986), p. 19. It is a matter of indisputable fact that the Reagan Administration has *not* funded the US Navy "at the expense" of other capabilities. At the close of the Carter Administration the Navy had 38% of the defense budget (to the Army's 28%), while for FY 1986 the Navy percentage is 35% (to the Army's 27.5%). Komer, *ibid.,* also misunderstands the rationale for horizontal escalation. He states: "The core of my argument is that winning consolation prizes like Cuba, Nicaragua, Angola, Ethiopia, or South Yemen would be utterly inadequate compensation for the loss of far more vital areas to Soviet landpower." Aside from the tautology in his argument, one can only say, first, "Amen," and second, ask, "who is making claims to the contrary?"

maritime assets could not be employed in the course of a short European campaign so as to have a truly major impact on the Central Front. There is nothing very surprising about this: British naval power could not intervene directly to thwart the execution of the Schlieffen Plan in August-September 1914, the Ludendorff Offensive of March 1918, or the unfolding of the Manstein Plan in May 1940.

Third, if NATO's ground and tactical air forces can remain in the field somewhere in Western Europe, US and allied naval power would play an essential role in NATO's military recovery — through provision of working control of the SLOCs and, increasingly, through flexibility in sea-based power projection (nautical maneuver) against a Soviet imperium that is vulnerable to attack on many geographical axes. Some proponents and critics of the Maritime Strategy have tended to debate the strategy out of its appropriate operational context. US and allied naval power is not going to save NATO-Europe in the event of a catastrophe, May 1940–style, on the Central Front. Sensible proponents of the case for the importance of Western maritime preponderance do not claim otherwise.

Fourth, US working control of the relevant lines of maritime communications will be essential whether or not a Soviet ground-forces' offensive can be held in Central Europe. Although from an American perspective, a war in Europe might be a vital campaign, it need not comprise *the war*—and it is very important for deterrence that Soviet leaders understand this point. Always assuming the functioning of strategic nuclear counterdeterrence, in the event of US military expulsion from continental Europe the US Navy again would assume its historic role of being the first line of the nation's defense.

Fifth, the contemporary US debate over the Maritime Strategy *allegedly* versus a continental strategy misses the point that the debate should not be over the relative merits of landpower or sea-power in US national military strategy. The United States cannot be a landpower beyond North America unless she is a seapower, and seapower has strategic meaning insofar as it has influence on events on land. There are, of course, very important force-structural and operational questions meriting debate that have to do with the detailed character of the fleet and how it should be fought in carefully specified circumstances.

Altogether there is today in the United States an imprudent obsession with one, admittedly important, problem — the difficulty of holding and repelling a Soviet ground assault in Central Europe. The United States must strive to keep the Soviet Union essentially landlocked, and strategically distracted from the full-fledged exercise of (maritime) *Weltpolitik* by continental security problems such as NATO in the West, China in the East, unstable clients in Eastern Europe, and fanatical Moslems to the South. However, the acknowledgment that the cutting edge of Soviet military power lies in its ground forces, should not translate into an argument for a stronger US Army and tactical air force at the expense of the US Navy. These points will bear repetition:

1. The prospect of protracted armed conflict should prove particularly deterring to the Soviet Union.[15] The entry price the United States must pay in order to threaten plausibly to impose such a conflict comprises a very convincing strategic nuclear counterdeterrent, and general preponderance at sea (though not, course, preponderance everywhere at sea).[16]
2. It would be vastly preferable for the Soviet Union to confront the prospect of a protracted conflict with a US bridgehead intact in continental NATO-Europe. Still, the case for a US Navy able to ensure US use of maritime communications for transportation and for power projection is equally strong, whether or not the protracted conflict includes an active continental NATO-European dimension.
3. The argument that the US Navy could destroy the Soviet surface and submarine fleet, and yet still contribute not at all to the defense of NATO'S Central Front, is a popular trivialization of strategy discussion.[17] The same point could have been made

---

[15] See Colin S. Gray, *Protracted War: The Lessons of History* (Fairfax, VA: National Institute for Public Policy, 1984).

[16] For an argument of timeless value on the meaning of command of the sea and what it permits, see Corbett, *Some Principles of Maritime Strategy,* Part II, Chapter 1.

[17] Guilty parties include Komer, *Maritime Strategy or Coalition Defense,* Chapter 7 (particularly pp. 67–68); and Luttwak, *The Pentagon and the Art of War,* pp. 111, 261–64. Some of the roots of Komer's misunderstanding of the character and value of maritime power are revealed in his brief and inaccurate treatment of the contribution of the British Royal Navy to victory in 1914–18, pp. 43–44. Komer, and others of his persuasion, would benefit from Richard Hough, *The Great War at Sea, 1914–1918* (Oxford: Oxford University Press, 1983).

with reference to Admiral Jellicoe's Grand Fleet of 1914, with equal lack of cogency. Only ready, deployed, or rapidly transportable ground and tactical air forces can preclude a Soviet *Blitzkrieg* victory in a one-to-two-week war in Central Western Europe. US and allied maritime power is not obviously relevant to this mission. The case for very strong US naval forces is: (a) to ensure that US reinforcements arrive rapidly so as to avoid a short war defeat for NATO; (b) to keep NATO "in the field" in a war that lasts more than a few weeks; (c) to exploit Soviet weaknesses on its flanks in a protracted war; (d) to apply pressure on the Soviet Union for war termination through the sinking of more and more of its strategic submarine (SSBN) force; (e) to enable the United States to wage a protracted war in Asia and Africa should Europe fall; and (f) truly *in extremis,* to contest a siege of the Americas if the Soviet Union should achieve hegemony over Eurasia and set about the translation of her superior continental landpower into a challenge for (selectively local) maritime superiority.

As happens not infrequently in defense debates, the orientation towards particular disagreements over naval force posture, operational deployment, and missions (e.g., over large carriers versus small carriers, power projection versus sea control), clouds the debate over national military strategy. From the public literature of the mid-1980s, one could derive the impression that the case for and against a 600-ship US Navy with fifteen carrier task forces hangs critically upon the answers to such questions as these: Should the Navy promptly assault the home bastions of Soviet naval power in the event of war? And, could success on "the flanks" contribute vitally to the defense of NATO's Central Front? This is a classic example of the wrong questions generating, necessarily, irrelevant answers.

NATO and the United States cannot sensibly choose between strength at sea and strength for the holding of Western Europe on land. NATO cannot hold on land if it cannot control its trans-Atlantic SLOC. A maritime strategy is mandated for the United States by reason of the geography of its competition with the Soviet Union. Some critics of US naval augmentation and modernization reduce the hypothetical future war almost strictly to a brief campaign for an initial (and possibly definitive) decision in Central Europe, neglecting to consider what might happen next. To be fair, or perhaps to spread the blame, proponents of the Maritime Strategy who choose to place emphasis upon the (very) short-war contribution of the US Navy, feed and invite continuation of this error.

Given the strong plausibility of the propositions that the ability to sustain a protracted global conflict may be critically important for the deterrence of war, and that nuclear counterdeterrence renders protracted US-Soviet armed conflict very probable indeed—*whether or not NATO holds in Western Europe*—several *caveats* must be noted concerning the development and operational uses of naval power.

First, the Western Alliance as a whole obviously should not construct a maritime-overbalanced reply to what is, in the first instance, essentially a landpower threat. However, it does not follow from this elementary point that the United States should not have a maritime-heavy orientation in its general purpose forces.[18]

Second, US and NATO maritime power should not be used in such a way as to enhance the prospect of a precipitate rate of vertical escalation.[19] For the enhancement of pre-war deterrence it is important that Soviet leaders should anticipate their Western foes being willing to adopt any and all means necessary to defeat Soviet strategy. Those means include endeavors to exploit differences of interest and commitment within the Soviet empire, denial of any absolute sanctuary status to Soviet home territory, and willingness to use nuclear weapons. In operational practice, however, the United States and Great Britain, preeminently though not necessarily exclusively within NATO, may choose to accord Soviet territory sanctuary status in order to minimize the risks to American and British territory. *If* Murmansk and Vladivostok were to be assaulted fairly promptly, Soviet leaders would have good grounds for replying against Norfolk, San Diego, and Portsmouth. Assuming that the initial blows against Murmansk and Vladivostok were non-nuclear

---

[18] This argument is advanced ably in Record, *Revising US Military Strategy*.

[19] Pertinent discussion is provided in Linton F. Brooks, "Escalation and Naval Strategy," *Proceedings*, vol. 110/8/978 (August 1984), pp. 33–37. The dangers of nuclear escalation at sea are well advertised, and indeed over-emphasized, in: Barry R. Posen, "Inadvertent Nuclear War? Escalation and NATO's Northern Flank," *International Security*, vol. 7, no. 2 (Fall 1982), pp. 28–54; and Desmond Ball, "Nuclear War at Sea," *International Security*, vol. 10, no. 3 (Winter 1985/86), pp. 3–31.

in character, it is worth recalling that the Soviet Union could find it technically very difficult to effect a similarly non-nuclear reply. In general, one should add, strategic defense deployments by the United States and NATO could assist greatly in helping to enforce escalation discipline.

Lest there be any misunderstanding, the second *caveat* reflects no more than a concern for due consideration in planning and force execution. Certainly it does not assume that assaults against the Soviet coasts must be unwise under all circumstances, or that freedom of choice necessarily will rest with the United States. However, this *caveat* does not assume that US maritime strategy is committed to an immediate offensive against the coastal bastions of Soviet seapower, regardless of strategic conditions or tactical circumstance. As Admiral Watkins has written:

> Early forward movement of carrier battle forces provides prudent positioning of our forces in order to support the requirements of the unified commanders and to roll back Soviet forces, should war come. It does not imply some immediate ''Charge of the Light Brigade'' attack on the Kola Peninsula or any other specific target. [20]

As suggested already, even if the essence of strategy, or perhaps of the quality required of a strategist, is the moral courage to make difficult choices, the real scope for strategic choice in US national military strategy is more limited than frequently is acknowledged. Contrasting historical examples of choices would be the correct US decision to abandon the Philippines in December 1941, and the incorrect British decision in January and February 1942 to allow their December 1941 determination to reinforce Singapore to stand (the 17th Indian and 18th British infantry divisions, which would have been invaluable in Burma, were sacrificed in a plainly lost cause, largely because Churchill was not prepared to brave Australian wrath.) If the United States continues down the path of global containment, geostrategic and political considerations serve vastly to narrow the scope for US innovation in strategy. In principle, the United States could choose to emphasize in her national military strategy:

1. Strategic forces (offensive and defensive);

---

[20] Watkins, ''The Maritime Strategy,'' in Watkins et al., *The Maritime Strategy*, p. 10.

2. Landpower;
3. Seapower.

A STRATEGIC FORCES' ORIENTATION

In practice, the requisite superiority, or military advantage for escalation dominance, literally may not be achieveable through strategic forces. Moreover, for good or ill, since the latter part of the
1960s the United States explicitly has eschewed strategic superiority
— the basis in the 1950s for extended nuclear deterrence — as a
strategic policy objective. The SDI might serve to restore some
genuine US strategic-force advantage if weaponized in multi-layer
form and married to strategic offensive forces modernized to defeat
emerging Soviet actual defenses. But it would be prudent for
American planners and commentators in the 1980s to recognize the
plain aversion in Western political culture to such a bid for the
restoration of superiority, as well as the improbability of its technical
accomplishment under current, peacetime circumstances.

So long as the United States lacks the ability to limit the level
of damage that it might suffer at home as a consequence of nuclear
operations that escalated out of a theater conflict, US strategic forces
must be relegated to the status of shield, and not sword, of the
Republic. This shield role is critical and entirely indispensable. In
effect, US strategic forces, whatever the balance as between offense
and defense in the posture, can function usefully in war fairly strictly
as a counterdeterrent. Those forces should be capable of denying
Soviet leaders any attractive options for escalating out of a stalemated or losing theater, or more likely multi-theater, campaign(s),
in search of victory through the functional equivalent of a Napoleonic "decisive battle" in the homeland-to-homeland mode.

This is not to suggest that a strategic-nuclear standoff does not
cast a shadow over local and theater conflict, inclining combatants
to caution lest Clausewitz' "grammar of war"[21] and "friction"[22]
produce a combat slide to an undesired scale of violence. But it is
to suggest that the "generous margin" of strength that the American
geopolitical theorist Nicholas Spykman claimed to be necessary for

---

[21] Clausewitz, *On War,* p. 605.
[22] Ibid., pp. 119–21.

a "positive foreign policy," is unlikely to be secured through improvements in strategic forces.[23] Spykman, writing in 1942, spoke of the value of "a margin of force which can be freely used." In terms of an objective analysis of the strategic balance, though not in terms of contemporary US political perception, the aircraft of SAC and of the US Navy provided such a margin in the 1950s. The prospects for restoration of US freedom of action *vis à vis* its strategic forces must be judged to be dim.

A LANDPOWER FOCUS

There is a cluster of strategic luminaries who claim that: (a) there is, at best, a stand-off in the balance of US-Soviet strategic forces; (b) Western maritime power is, and will remain, greatly superior to Soviet maritime power, but that the Soviet empire, unlike the Japanese empire, is not at all vulnerable to maritime pressure (the USSR does not have important SLOCs, vulnerable and valuable insular possessions, coasts with easy access to seaborne assault, located close to the centers of national power, and so on); and (c) that therefore, in the words of Edward Luttwak, "the ground-forces divisions are the basic currency of East-West strategy."[24]

Not for the first time, indeed really for the third time—previous ventures being in 1951–52 and 1961–65—some postwar US strategists, official and unofficial, are repeating what Sir Douglas Haig told Lloyd George in 1916–18 and what George Marshall told Churchill in 1942–44: there is no effective alternative to meeting the continental superpower enemy with landpower in the principal theater of operations, i.e., on the ground in Europe. Four generic difficulties beset the advocates of a heavy continental-landpower orientation to US national military strategy.

First, in preparing so substantially for nearly the worst case event (the absolutely worst case event would be a Soviet preventive nuclear assault on the continental United States) of a Soviet attack in Europe, the United States would risk being severely deficient in flexible, prudently usable military power relevant to most other

[23] Spykman, *America's Strategy in World Politics*, p. 21.
[24] Luttwak, *The Pentagon and the Art of War*, p. 120 (see also p. 64). Lest there be any misperception, I would like to register the highest admiration for Edward Luttwak as a strategic thinker, *save* on the subjects of landpower-seapower and military reform.

insecurity scenarios around Rimland Eurasia. US policymakers would be doing the reverse of capitalizing upon US geostrategic strengths were they to lock up more and more military power in, and committed to, a European garrison.

Second, proponents of a continentalist-landpower focus should not be permitted, in the excitement of debate, to neglect the point that the continent most in question is an ocean away. If the war is decided in Europe in 5–10 days with minimum — or, more likely, less — notice for counter-mobilization, then SLOC protection and support of NATO's flanks may well be close to irrelevant. But, what if the war is not over in 5–10 days? More to the point perhaps, what if NATO fares poorly in the field, but the US President wishes to continue the war where he can? This second point must be extended beyond the reminder that US landpower overseas must rest upon working control of the seas, to include the *caveat* that a Soviet enemy either thwarted on land or so successful on land that he fears US/NATO nuclear initiatives in desperation, will need to be discouraged from launching preventive/preemptive nuclear attacks.

Third, as Richard Betts has argued, conventional deterrence cannot be regarded as entirely reliable.[25] One must add, somewhat hastily, that no form of deterrence can be thoroughly reliable. Notwithstanding the apparent fact that conventional deterrence is strengthened very usefully by the awesome nuclear dangers that loom over it, one cannot ignore the point that robust conventional capabilities may, on balance, have the undesired effect of reducing deterrence. Substantial ramparts of non-nuclear stopping power necessarily must flag a NATO intention to attempt a non-nuclear defense. There is much to recommend such a course, but proponents of a thoroughly non-nuclear defense have to face the possible problems that: they may be offering the Soviet Union, or encouraging Soviet belief that it has, a non-nuclear option for theater war and, thereby, may be reducing seriously the risks that Soviet leaders anticipate as they consider military adventure; and that a very successful non-nuclear defense could well motivate the Soviet Union to escalate in a quest for victory by other means and in other climes.

[25] Richard K. Betts, "Conventional Deterrence: Predictive Uncertainty and Policy Confidence," *World Politics*, vol. 37, no. 2 (January 1985), pp. 153–79; and "Compound Deterrence vs. No-First-Use: What's Wrong is What's Right," *Orbis*, vol. 28, no. 4 (Winter 1985), pp. 697–718.

History is replete with cases of the failure of conventional deterrence. Such deterrence undoubtedly is different, to a degree, between nuclear-armed adversaries, as contrasted with non-nuclear coalitions. Nonetheless, it would be prudent to be alert to the dangerous possibility that the benefit to NATO of a military condition wherein very early resort to nuclear weapons would not be essential, may have to be paid for in the coin of some diminution in overall deterrent effect.

Fourth, it is very far from certain that a US continental-land-power reorientation would "work." In theory there is no difficulty translating the economic assets of NATO into designs for conventional forces, strategy, operational art, and tactics — but practice could be very different. It is worth mentioning the point that one is not only in the realm of speculative theory with regard to the probability of NATO actually fielding a truly robust conventional defense. There is, after all, nearly forty years of continuous coalition experience. That experience has to suggest to an unprejudiced observer that the prospects of NATO purchasing and then sustaining a quantity and quality of military power suitable to offset the Soviet ground forces, on their own terms, are not overly good. At the very least, given the fate of the "Lisbon goals" of 1952, of the Kennedy version of flexible response in the 1960s, and of the Carter Administration/NATO 1978 Long-Term Defense Program (LTDP), it is not unreasonable to say that the burden of proof rests upon those who argue that NATO can field a very robust conventional deterrent.

This fourth point has two distinct dimensions, the general military and the political. The latter dimension refers to the fact that there are severe limits to what the US Army could achieve for the defense of Central Europe, virtually no matter how well favored it was to be in terms of relative funding preference in the defense budget. Forward defense on the Central Front is a coalition enterprise. While the US Seventh Army can improve its ability to defend its two corps areas, there are very practical limits to the extent to which improvements in the "fighting power" of US ground forces can substitute for major deficiencies on the part of allies. The US Congress, one may be certain, would not permit an augmentation of the US ground defense role in Europe.

Major questions pertain to the feasibility of NATO fielding a truly reliable conventional "war-fighting" deterrent in Central Europe. US "military reformers" and others have been rediscovering the wheel in recent years (e.g., the very ambiguous and much abused concept of maneuver),[26] and have been seeking inspiration in somewhat romanticized interpretations of the performance of the German Army on the Eastern Front,[27] in Normandy, and on the frontiers of the Reich on the Siegfried Line. The purpose of this discussion is not to distinguish the more from the less plausible ways in which NATO's landpower might be developed and employed effectively. Instead, the purpose here is to suggest that the current criticism of US maritime strategy does not rest self-evidently upon a fully persuasive landpower story.

The ranks of continental-landpower strategists contain advocates of: *field fortification* (after the Siegfried, not the Maginot, Line), undampened by the political rejection of this option by the Federal Republic of Germany; new *"emerging technologies" (ET)*, though the critical distinction between weapon and force survivability continues to elude many; ET-related (dependent) ideas of *deep-strike and follow-on forces attack* (FOFA), which probably would be an exceedingly expensive way of attempting that which military history suggests to be incapable of having decisive effect; *maneuver,* an idea as old as war itself which has come to assume near-mystical significance in the reformers' credo, notwithstanding the politically-mandated maldeployment of NATO's more mobile, "maneuver" ground assets, the absence of "maneuver forces" in deep theater reserve, and the inconvenient fact of a lack of geographical depth in the theater. There is much to be said in favor of all of these elements—fortification, new technology, interdiction, and maneuver—but, severally or in combination, they do not yield anything even close to a guarantee of successful defense.[28] Utilizing deception for surprise, and then attempting disruption of the NATO front through deep armored/mechanized penetration and widespread

---

[26] See William S. Lind, *Maneuver Warfare Handbook* (Boulder, CO: Westview, 1985). A thought-provoking critique of the military reformers is Richard K. Betts, "Conventional Strategy: New Critics, Old Choices," *International Security,* vol. 7, no. 4 (Spring 1983), pp. 140–62.

[27] See Dennis E. Showalter, "A Dubious Heritage: The Military Legacy of the Russo-German War," *Air University Review,* vol. 36, no. 3 (March-April 1985), pp. 4–23.

[28] The difficulty of judging how well NATO might fare "on the night" is well illustrated in Barry R. Posen, "Measuring the European Conventional Balance: Coping with Complexity in Threat Assessment," *International Security,* vol. 9, no. 3 (Winter 1984/85), pp. 47–88.

Spetsnaz and airborne force employment, Warsaw Pact forces *might* achieve an unraveling of NATO's defenses so devastating at the outset of a war that recovery would be improbable. This is not a prediction, but it is asserted here as a distinct possibility that requires frank recognition if those who argue in a landpower versus seapower mode, in favor of the former, are to answered suitably.

On both political and military grounds, the case for the United States continuing to make a continental landpower commitment to Europe is a strong one. Nonetheless, advocates of a greater US landpower contribution to NATO in Europe, albeit for the best of motives, are encouraging US policy to move in the wrong direction. The task of defending NATO-European territory on the ground should be a mission primarily, *and increasingly,* entrusted to Europeans. NATO-European countries, now long-recovered from the ravages of World War II, should not be treated as wards of Washington, but rather as allies. These European allies need to believe that, to the degree feasible, their destiny is in their own hands. Moreover, if Americans are to remain tolerably content with their entangling alliance connection with Europe, it is most important that the terms of implementation of that connection be judged to be just. In short, Europeans should be seen to do as much as they are able towards their own defense—not merely as little as they deem consistent with US Congressional tolerance. US society should not be assessed by Americans to be at very early nuclear risk for reason of allied unwillingness to provide the locally affordable means of sustaining a non-nuclear defense.[29]

Detailed consideration of the purposes and character of the US continental commitment to NATO-Europe, appraised in the context both of the prospects for success in the land battle and of the political evolution of the alliance, transcends the mandate of this analysis.

A MARITIME EMPHASIS

Here, as in the discussion of "a landpower focus," the subject is the focus or emphasis *for the United States,* not for the Western Alliance as whole. It should go without saying that the most serious

---

[29] See Earl C. Ravenal, "Counterforce and Alliance: The Ultimate Connection," *International Security,* vol. 6, no. 4 (Spring 1982), pp. 26–43.

strategic problem facing NATO-Europe is the possibility of invasion by Warsaw Pact ground forces, and that that problem has to be met on its own terms. But, given the very great economic strength of Washington's Eurasian allies, it does not go without saying that continental campaigning *à la* Eisenhower should be the principal emphasis in, or contemplated end-product of, US general-purpose force planning.

A war in Europe could be lost not only in Europe, but also indirectly as a consequence of an interrupted trans-Atlantic SLOC, and through Soviet ability to swing forces from the Chinese frontier to the European theater (as Stalin did with many of his divisions from Siberia and Central Asia in November-December 1941). Furthermore, in circumstances short of war in Europe, the US-organized alliance structure in Europe and Asia would be placed under potentially fatal strain were the Soviet Union able to deny the West (and Japan) access to Gulf oil. Oil from that region is by no means of critical significance for the United States, but it is vital for the economies of many of its major allies.

If the territorial security of Western Europe could be defended only by a much augmented and modernized US Army and by US tactical air power, then there would be a strong case for reorienting US military investment. However, plainly that is not, and will not be, the situation. Indeed, it is no exaggeration to say that the very strong emphasis placed upon the forward NATO commitment by the Carter Administration reflected not so much a careful appraisal of US national military strategy, but rather a political belief that, in the aftermath of Vietnam, the NATO track was relatively non-controversial in the US Congress.

This author eschews acceptance of a "maritime" or a "continentalist" affiliation as those misleading labels have been employed of recent years. War against a great continental power cannot be won, though it can be lost, at sea. The US armed forces should be "balanced" both with reference to capabilites provided by the alliance as a whole, and with regard to prospective commitment in pursuit of the specific objectives into which US vital interests translate. Those forces should not be "balanced" as by some astrategic algorithm of "fair shares" for the separate services, or without reference to the existence of front-line allies who, one must presume, are even more interested in deterring or repelling geographically contiguous Soviet landpower than is the United States.

Endorsement of a maritime emphasis in US national military strategy — with its proper expression in force structure — does not mean that one: is blind to the landpower character of the Soviet threat to the territorial integrity of NATO-Europe; fails to recognize the relative inaccessibility of much of the Soviet imperium to pressure from the sea; or that one is determined to hazard US carrier task forces in very severely contested areas on the Soviet maritime frontier at the very outset of a war. The case for a maritime emphasis in US national military strategy rests upon the following considerations, to risk repeating themes introduced in this discussion already:

1. Recognition that it is politically essential and militarily efficient for NATO-Europe to provide the overwhelming majority of the ready and rapidly mobilizable ground forces for local defense.
2. Recognition of the fact that working control of key SLOCs would be absolutely essential if NATO were to be able to sustain a conflict in Europe, and/or if the United States were to prosecute a more protracted war — regardless of how the campaign in Europe had developed.
3. Recognition of the likely global character, or certain global *potential*, of a protracted conflict, and of the importance of providing such strategically useful distraction on the very far-flung flanks of Soviet power as could be achieved at tolerable cost. If NATO can hold, if with great difficulty, in the center, it will begin to be very important indeed that Soviet leaders should feel pressed in the far North, in Southern Europe, and — above all — generally feel over-extended in the European theater of operations as a consequence both of US operations in the Northeast Pacific and of the (probably latent) Chinese threat that flanks their entire position in the East.
4. Appreciation of the fact that although the benchmark for adequacy in military preparation would be provided by the test of battle in the event of a Soviet invasion,[30] the United States and

---

[30] "The decision by arms is for all major and minor operations in war what cash payment is in commerce. Regardless how complex the relationship between the two parties, regardless how rarely settlements actually occur, they can never be entirely absent." Clausewitz, *On War*, p. 97.

her allies are operating day by day in a condition of war in peace. There are few security problems in peacetime to which US naval power is not more or less relevant. Always assuming an adequate framework for the deterrence of major war in Europe, the real action in East-West security relations through the year 2000 will involve regional problems and, both for political and military reasons, US naval forces will comprise the lion's share of, as well as the *sine qua non* for, Washington's response. (This is not to deny that the willingness of US public opinion to commit armed forces in regional conflict will fluctuate over time.) The proliferation of military high-technology in the third world means that a US naval task force capable of operating against Soviet maritime power in the North Atlantic may not be greatly over-designed if it is to function reliably in regional conflict.

5

CONCLUSIONS: THE UTILITY AND LIMITATIONS OF SEAPOWER

The argument developed in this monograph, if it was competently done, should have gored the oxen of several schools of thought on US national military strategy. It has been argued here that:

- NATO's strategy of flexible response, at least as currently expressed in plans and forces, places an imprudently heavy burden on the scarcely credible, or militarily useful, prospect of controlled nuclear escalation (within and beyond the European region).
- While the non-nuclear defense of NATO-Europe can and should be improved, there are probably quite severe constraints on the level of improvement that is feasible. Most of that improvement should be effected by European countries rather than by the United States. At the least, it is very unwise to have NATO's short-war stopping power critically dependent on very prompt arrival of US reinforcements.
- Unless the US SDI is able to produce some close facsimile of a leakproof "astrodome," and the Soviet strategic defense network cannot, Western policymakers should have the courage of their innermost convictions and cease pretending that it is the 1950s

rather than the 1980s and come to terms, carefully and slowly, with the strategic policy obsolescence of the concept of extended nuclear deterrence. The victim of the fiction that vertical (nuclear) escalation would be the order of the day in the event of military setbacks in the attempted defense of NATO-Europe is not a Soviet Government that is usefully misled by the bluff, but rather a Western Alliance which continues to live in a security edifice that could not withstand really severe weather.

■ Nuclear deemphasis for the United States and its allies, if sensibly considered, is no longer a matter of choice. Fortunately, the global maritime alliance led by the United States has a markedly superior option as an alternative to the nuclear crutch. In principle at least, the West has the political, economic, and geostrategic assests, bound together and sustained by superior maritime strength, to compel the unstable empire of the Soviet Union, with its potentially very fractious minorities at home, and its sullen, even hostile, satellites abroad, to wage a prolonged non-nuclear war that Moscow should not anticipate being able to win.

In this monograph the author has sought to be careful not to promise, or even appear to promise, political or strategic miracles that would solve the problems of national security policy at a stroke. Even readers who are not sympatheic to the argument should concede that the discussion recognizes, *inter alia:* the difficulty of translating superior seapower into power of favorable decision on land; the distinct possibility that NATO may not hold on the Central Front, which means that the global strategic context for the maritime investment of the Soviet imperial fortress would be greatly affected to the US disadvantage; and, finally, the residual risk of vertical (nuclear) escalation can never be thoroughly removed, no matter what US, or Soviet, pre-war strategic policy intentions might be.

Two decades ago Admiral Wylie notice that "there has been too little disciplined effort made to study warfare in its totality. . . ."[1] The Admiral proceeded to observe that soldiers, sailors, and airmen, "by and large . . . do not recognize that they are following, and are indeed bound by, definite theories."[2] The US defense policy debate in the 1980s is very much in the condition just specified.

---

[1] Wylie, *Military Strategy,* p. 31.
[2] Ibid., p. 32.

There are sub-communities of strategic-forces/central war, European-continentalist/NATO's Central Front, and maritime theorists and practitioners, who are pursuing their separate trades with scant effective recognition of the essential, and certainly potential, unity of all their individual concerns.

A maritime emphasis in US strategy is favored here because, in the words of an honest American soldier, Major Glenn M. Harned, commenting on the US Navy's current Maritime Strategy:

> It correctly takes into account the United States' position as a global maritime power, not a Eurasian continental power.[3]

Major Harned proceeded into dangerous waters, or perhaps a minefield, by adding that:

> Some Army opposition to the Maritime Strategy occurs because the Army lacks a corresponding "Continental Strategy" for the conduct of strategic air-land operations within the context of a global war with the Soviet Union. The Army's planning and programming suffer for the lack of a coherent global strategy.[4]

The Major is wrong, albeit for the right reason of a praiseworthy desire for strategic coherence. The US Army does not require a "continental strategy." The last thing the United States needs to do is to emulate the historical experiences of Great Britain and Imperial Germany in the years preceding the First World War. In that period British and German soldiers and sailors each contentedly pursued distinctive, non-synergistic, service strategy designs. Since strategic geography mandates that Soviet power can be repelled or brought down only on land, but that US landpower can be rendered strategically effective only if transported and sustained by sea (one should recall the old saying that for a maritime power the Army is a bullet fired by the navy), it should be plain that the US armed services require an inclusive and non-service sectarian theory of war.

The strategy challenge for American theorists and planners is to devise methods and instruments of war that play to US and general Western strengths and to Soviet vulnerabilities. Moreover, those

---

[3] Major Glenn M. Harned, "Comment and Discussion: 'The Maritime Strategy'," *Proceedings*, vol. 112/2/996 (February 1986), p. 26.
[4] Ibid.

methods and instruments must include very strong fences against Soviet inclinations to change the rules of engagement in their favor. While NATO must strive to remain "in the field" in the event of a Soviet invasion of Europe, it is also very important, perhaps critical for deterrence, that Soviet leaders should not be convinced that they would be able to wage the war that they prefer, according to plan — that is to say a short non-nuclear war confined to Western Europe. There is nothing very controversial in Admiral Watkin's judgment that:

> The probable centerpiece of Soviet strategy in global war would be a combined arms assault against Europe, where they would seek a quick and decisive victory. As prudent military planners, the Soviets would, of course, prefer to be able to concentrate on a single theater; *a central premise of US strategy is to deny them such an option.* (Emphasis added.)[5]

It is most fitting that this discussion should close on a cautionary note, with an historical example that shows the limitations as well as the strategic utility of seapower, and which—above all else— shows the interdependency of seapower and landpower. In his classic study of the Trafalgar campaign, Sir Julian Corbett argued as follows:

> By universal assent Trafalgar is ranked as one of the decisive battles of the world, and yet of all the great victories there is not one which to all appearances was so barren of immediate result. It had brought to a triumphant conclusion one of the most masterly and complex sea campaigns in history, but in so far as it was an integral part of the combined campaign (with actions on land) its results are scarcely to be discerned. It gave to England finally the dominion of the seas, but it left Napoleon dictator of the Continent. So incomprehensible was its apparent sterility that to fill the void a legend grew up that it saved England from invasion.[6]

Corbett then proceeds to explain how the combination of Napoleon's genius *on land* (he was at the height of his competence) and the military incapacity of the Third Coalition in the years 1805–1807, served to limit the benefits that might, and perhaps

---

[5] Watkins, "The Maritime Strategy," p. 7.
[6] Corbett, *The Campaign of Trafalgar,* p. 408.

should, have flowed from Nelson's victory on October 21, 1805. He concludes his study with the following judgments:

> It was not merely that it [the campaign of Trafalgar] secured the British Isles from invasion. The ramparts it built stretched to the ends of the earth. It was not merely that it destroyed the French naval power. By securing bases in the Mediterranean and towards the East, it made it impossible for any partial revival of Napoleon's navy to place any part of our overseas possessions in serious jeopardy. Against any other man than Napoleon, with another ally than Prussia as she then was, it might well have done much more. As it was the sea had done all that the sea could do, and for Europe the end was failure.[7]

Superior seapower, protected by a sufficient strategic-nuclear counterdeterrent, is a prerequisite for the basic national security of an insular contemporary United States, as it was for the Britain of the Napoleonic era and well beyond. Then as now, however, success at sea needs to be married to competence on land. If she is fortunate — in the calamitous circumstances of a massive failure of deterrence — the United States will find the military destiny of her Soviet adversary commanded by persons less inspired than was the Napoleon of 1805–1807, and the performance of her allies considerably more determined and skillful than was that of the Austria that went down to defeat at Austerlitz on December 2, 1805, or the Prussia that was defeated at Jena-Auerstadt on October 14, 1806.

---

[7] Ibid., p. 424. There is an interesting ambiguity in the final sentence quoted. For many years following the victory at Trafalgar in October 1805, unchallengeable British seapower did fail to save Europe from Napoleonic hegemony. But, ultimately, through the effects of the blockade, British seapower was the prime cause of Napoleon's downfall.

National Strategy Information Center, Inc.

PUBLICATIONS IN PRINT

William C. Bodie, Editor

AGENDA PAPERS

Natural Resources in Soviet Foreign Policy by John R. Thomas, September 1985

Military Doctrine and the American Character: Reflections on AirLand Battle by Herbert I. London, November 1984

The United States and the Persian Gulf: Past Mistakes, Present Needs by Alvin J. Cottrell and Michael Moodie, May 1984

The China Sea: The American Stake in its Future by Harold C. Hinton, January 1981

NATO, Turkey, and the Southern Flank: A Mideastern Perspective by Ihsan Gürkan, March 1980

The Soviet Threat to NATO's Northern Flank by Marian K. Leighton, November 1979

Power Projection: A Net Assessment of U.S. and Soviet Capabilities by W. Scott Thompson, April 1978

Seven Tracks to Peace in the Middle East by Frank R. Barnett, April 1975

Can We Avert Economic Warfare in Raw Materials? US Agriculture as a Blue Chip by William Schneider, Jr., July 1974

STRATEGY PAPERS

Labor in Soviet Global Strategy by Roy Godson, May 1984

The Soviet Control Structure: Capabilities for Wartime Survival by Harriet Fast Scott and William F. Scott, September 1983

Strategic Weapons: An Introduction by Norman Polmar, October 1975. Revised edition, June 1982

Soviet Perceptions of Military Doctrine and Military Power: The Interaction of Theory and Practice by John J. Dziak, June 1981

How Little is Enough? SALT and Security in the Long Run by Francis P. Hoeber, January 1981

Raw Material Supply in a Multipolar World by Yuan-li Wu, October 1973. Revised edition, October 1979

India: Emergent Power? by Stephen P. Cohen and Richard L. Park, June 1978

The Evolution of Soviet Security Strategy 1965-1975 by Avigdor Haselkorn, November 1977

Food, Foreign Policy, and Raw Materials Cartels by William Schneider, Jr., February 1976

Soviet Sources of Military Doctrine and Strategy by William F. Scott, July 1975

The Soviet Presence in Latin America by James D. Theberge, June 1974

The Horn of Africa by J. Bowyer Bell, Jr., December 1973

Research and Development and the Prospects for International Security by Frederick Seitz and Rodney W. Nichols, December 1973

BOOKS

Maritime Strategy, Geopolitics, and the Defense of the West by Colin S. Gray, August 1986

Bibliography on Soviet Intelligence and Security Services edited by Raymond G. Rocca and John J. Dziak, July 1985

Special Operations in US Strategy edited by Frank R. Barnett, B. Hugh Tovar, and Richard H. Shultz, January 1985

Dezinformatsia: Active Measures in Soviet Strategy by Richard H. Sultz and Roy Godson, March 1984

On the Brink: Defense, Deficits, and Welfare Spending by James L. Clayton, November 1983

U.S. International Broadcasting and National Security by James L. Tyson, November 1983

Arms, Men, and Military Budgets: Issues for Fiscal year 1981 by Francis P. Hoeber, William Schneider, Jr., Norman Polmar, and Ray Bessette, Mary 1980

Arms, Men, and Military Budgets: Issues for Fiscal Year 1979 by Francis P. Hoeber, David B. Kassing, and William Schneider, Jr., February 1978

Arms, Men, and Military Budgets: Issues for Fiscal Year 1978 edited by Francis P. Hoeber and William Schneider, Jr., May 1977

Arms, Men, and Military Budgets: Issues for Fiscal Year 1977 edited by William Schneider, Jr., and Francis P. Hoeber, May 1976

* * *

Intelligence Requirements for the 1980s: Intelligence and Policy (Volume VII of a Series) edited by Roy Godson, October 1985

Intelligence Requirements for the 1980s: Domestic Intelligence (Volume VI of a Series) edited by Roy Godson, October 1985

Intelligence Requirements for the 1980s: Clandestine Collection (Volume V of a Series) edited by Roy Godson, November 1982

Intelligence Requirements for the 1980s: Covert Action (Volume IV of a Series) edited by Roy Godson, September 1981

Intelligence Requirements for the 1980s: Counterintelligence (Volume III of a Series) edited by Roy Godson, January 1981

Intelligence Requirements for the 1980s: Analysis and Estimates (Volume II of a Series) edited by Roy Godson, June 1980

Intelligence Requirements for the 1980s: Elements of Intelligence (Volume I of a Series) edited by Roy Godson, October 1979

* * *

The Regionalization of Warfare edited by James Brown and William P. Snyder, June 1985

The Soviet View of U.S. Strategic Doctrine by Jonathan Samuel Lockwood, April 1983

Strategic Military Surprise: Incentives and Opportunities edited by Klaus Knorr and Patrick Morgan, January 1983

National Security Affairs: Theoretical Perspectives and Contemporary Issues edited by B. Thomas Trout and James E. Harf, October 1982

False Science: Underestimating the Soviet Arms Buildup by Steven Rosefielde, July 1982

Our Changing Geopolitical Premises by Thomas P. Rona, January 1982

U.S. Policy and Low-Intensity Conflict: Potentials for Military Struggles in the 1980s edited by Sam C. Sarkesian and William L. Scully, June 1981

The Fateful Ends and Shades of SALT: Past . . . Present . . . And Yet to Come? by Paul H. Nitze, James E. Dougherty, and Francis X. Kane, March 1979

Strategic Options for the Early Eighties: What Can Be Done? edited by William R. Van Cleave and W. Scott Thompson, February 1979

* * *

The Intelligent Layperson's Guide to "Star Wars" by Joyce E. Larson and William C. Bodie, July 1986

War and Peace: Soviet Russia Speaks edited by Albert L. Weeks and William C. Bodie, with an essay by Frank R. Barnett, March 1983